The Professional Programmers Guid

Ada

John Dawes
ICL Defence Systems

Pitman

PITMAN PUBLISHING
128 Long Acre London WC2E 9AN

First published in Great Britain 1988

British Library Cataloguing in Publication Data
Dawes, John
The professional programmers guide to
Ada.—(Professional programming guides).
1. Ada (Computer program language)
I. Title
005.13'3 QA76.73.A15
ISBN 0–273–02821–9

Printed and bound in Great Britain at The Bath Press, Avon

Contents

Preface

This book is intended as a handy reference guide to the Ada language for the use of experienced programmers with at least some knowledge of Ada.

The Ada language is defined in the Ada Language Reference Manual, ANSI/MIL-STD 1815A. The Reference Manual's main purpose is to define the language rigorously, and it is not always very convenient for reference by the principal users of the language – programmers.

In this book I have tried to present the whole Ada language in a convenient manner. The material is based on the Reference Manual, but I have drawn on the commentaries of the Ada Joint Program Office's Language Maintenance Panel in a few places where the Reference Manual is ambiguous or vague.

I am grateful to my colleagues at ICL Defence Systems and to the reviewers for their criticisms of a draft of the book; for all remaining errors (I cannot hope there are none) I am of course entirely responsible. I am grateful also to the Board of ICL Plc for permission to publish the book.

The specifications of the predefined packages and the collected syntax are reproduced from the Reference Manual by permission of the US Department of Defense Ada Joint Program Office.

John Dawes
ICL, 1988

1 Introduction

This book describes the Ada programming language, as defined in ANSI/MIL-STD 1815A (1983): Reference Manual for the Ada Programming Language.

The reader is assumed to be a programmer with at least a general knowledge of the Ada language, such as can be gained from an introductory text or course. The book is arranged for convenient reference, which has entailed a certain amount of repetition of information; to keep this within bounds some commonly occurring concepts are described here and referred to from the body of the book.

1.1 Notation

This mostly follows the Reference Manual: Ada reserved words are in **lower case bold**, identifiers in `UPPER_CASE`. The layout of examples follows the recommendations of the Reference Manual.

The collected syntax in Appendix D uses the conventions of the Reference Manual: syntactic categories in lower case; square brackets [ ] enclose optional items; braces { } enclose items repeated 0 or more times; and vertical bar | separates alternatives. Elsewhere common syntactic categories are represented by single upper case letters, and repetition is indicated by ellipsis:

`X; ...;` and `Y, ...`

meaning 1 or more of `X` each terminated by a semicolon, and 1 or more of `Y` separated by commas with no terminator.

1.2 Illegal and erroneous programs

Ada programs can suffer from errors of various kinds, which are classified and described in this book as follows.

(1) *Illegal programs* The syntactic or semantic rules of the language are broken in a way that a compiler can (and must) detect and reject. This book describes only legal programs, so that such phrases

as *must* and *must not* mean that a disobeying program is illegal.

(2) *Erroneous programs* The semantic rules of the program are broken in a way that a compiler may not be able to (and need not) detect. The word *erroneous* is always used to describe these errors.

(3) *Incorrect order dependences* The effect of a program depends on the order of certain executed actions whose order is not defined. A compiler is not expected to detect these. The phrase *in an undefined order* is always used for these cases.

(4) *Predefined exceptions* These are raised by the execution of the program when certain checks fail or other exceptional conditions occur. These possibilities are mentioned explicitly.

(5) *Logical errors* A program which is correct in all other respects may not do what was intended. Here the reader is on his or her own, as far as this book is concerned.

1.3 Implementation-dependent features

The Reference Manual allows some features to be wholly or partly omitted, or in some other way to depend on the implementation. Rules are laid down as to the degree of freedom that the implementor has in each case. These rules are not given here in any detail; a note is made of the implementation dependence, and a recommendation is given to consult your User's Guide (which should contain full details of all such features).

A number of important properties of the target machine can be found from the predefined package `SYSTEM` (section 16.2.2).

1.4 Attributes

Attributes supply various kinds of information about entities in the program. The general form is

`X'A` or `X'A(Z)`

where the prefix `X` denotes the entity, `A` is the name of the attribute, and `Z` if required is a parameter particular to the attribute. For example the statements

```
I := INTEGER'FIRST;
S := INTEGER'IMAGE(I);
```

assign the value of the first value of the type INTEGER to I; and a printable representation of it to the string S.

Language-defined attributes applicable to particular kinds of entities as prefixes are described in appropriate places in this book, and summarised in Appendix A. Additional attributes may be supported by particular Ada compilers, and should be defined in your User's Guide.

Attribute names have the form of identifiers, but are not reserved words or predefined identifiers. They may be used freely as identifiers without affecting their use as attributes (except for RANGE, DIGITS, and DELTA, which are also reserved words).

1.5 Pragmas

Pragmas are a means of controlling the action of the compiler or conveying information to it. A pragma has one of the forms

```
pragma  P;

pragma  P(A,...);
```

where P is the name of the pragma and the arguments A are expressions, given by the positional association or (if the pragma supports named arguments) by named association (section 1.7).

There are 14 *language-defined* pragmas, which are always supported, defined in appropriate places in the book and summarised in Appendix B. Other implementation-defined pragmas may be provided: consult your User's Guide. Any pragma that is not recognised, or which is in the wrong place or has the wrong number or kind of arguments, is ignored (except that a warning may be given).

Some language-defined pragmas (e.g. INTERFACE) allow special names as arguments; implementation-defined pragmas may do so also. These special names have only this meaning within the pragma; elsewhere they are normal identifiers.

Pragmas are in general allowed before, after or between all kinds of statements and declarations, and within certain compound statements. Particular pragmas have particular rules for their placing.

Pragma names have the form of identifiers but are not reserved words or predefined identifiers. They may be freely used as identifiers without affecting their use as pragmas.

1.6 Representation clauses

Many aspects of the mapping of entities declared in the program to the underlying machine can be influenced by the programmer by means of **representation clauses**. They are described in detail in the body of the book, and summarised in Appendix C. The following features are generally true.

(1) A representation clause must appear in the same package specification or declarative part as the declaration of the entity to which it applies, after the declaration but before any *forcing* occurrence of the name of the entity, i.e. an occurrence that forces the compiler to choose a representation for the entity. A **forcing occurrence** is:

- for a *type*, any occurrence of the type, any subtype of it, or any type having a component of that type, except:
  - as the type mark in a type, subtype, or deferred constant declaration
  - as the type of a formal parameter or the result in a subprogram specification or an entry declaration
  - in a pragma (if such an occurrence would otherwise be forcing, the pragma may be ignored)
  - in a representation clause for the type itself.
- for an *object*, any occurrence of its name is forcing.
- for a *program unit* or *entry*, only an occurrence in an address attribute `A'ADDRESS` is forcing.

(2) Only one representation clause of any one kind can be given for an entity.

(3) The effect of a representation clause is always to some extent implementation-dependent, and a compiler may impose restrictions on its use, even to the extent of not supporting it at all. Use of an unsupported representation clause is illegal.

1.7 Associations

These are used to associate expressions with objects. The form is

```
(A, ...)
```

where each association A is either just an expression E (a **positional association**) or else has the form

```
N | ... => E
```

(a **named association**). A named association with more than one name N is equivalent to a sequence of associations

```
N => E, ...
```

one for each name, with the expression E repeated for each.

The general rules are as follows.

(1) A named association associates the expression E with the named object N; a positional association associates it with the object in the corresponding position.

(2) Named associations can occur in any order, but if both kinds occur the positional associations must come first.

(3) Each object must have just one associated expression.

(4) A possible name N is **others**, on its own in the last association, and meaning all possible objects not already named.

Associations are used in *pragmas* (section 1.5), *discriminant constraints* (section 6.2.3), *aggregates* (sections 6.1.4, 6.2.7), *subprogram calls* (sections 12.1.3, 12.2.2), and *generic instantiations* (section 14.2).

1.8 Multiple declarations

A **multiple declaration** contains a list of more than one identifier

```
I, ...
```

In every case a multiple declaration is equivalent to a sequence of **single declarations**, one for each identifier in the list, in the same order, with the rest of the declaration repeated (so that any expressions are repeatedly evaluated). For instance

```
I, J, K : INTEGER range -F(N) .. F(N) := 0;
```

has exactly the same effect as

```
I : INTEGER range -F(N) .. F(N) := 0;
J : INTEGER range -F(N) .. F(N) := 0;
K : INTEGER range -F(N) .. F(N) := 0;
```

Multiple declarations are possible in *object declarations* (section 3.4.1), *component specifications* (section 6.2), *parameter specifications* (section 12.1.1), and *generic parameter specifications* (section 14.1).

1.9 Conformance

In a number of places in the language a construct has to be repeated; e.g. a subprogram specification in a subprogram declaration and in the corresponding subprogram body. The two occurrences need not be identical, but they must **conform**: they must consist of the same sequence of lexical elements (except for comments) with the following allowed equivalents:

(1) different numeric literals with the same type and value
(2) an *expanded name* (section 7.1) in place of an identifier, operator symbol, or character literal, from the same declaration
(3) different operator symbols denoting the same operator by *renaming* (section 3.2.5) .

Note that, because of (2), conformance is not transitive: `A` and `B.A` conform as do `A` and `C.A`, but `B.A` and `C.A` do not. `D.B.A` and `B.A` conform, however.

1.10 Program units and frames

The overall structure of an Ada program is defined in terms of **program units**. A program unit is one of the following

- a subprogram (procedure or function)
- a package
- a task unit
- a generic unit (generic subprogram or generic package)

A generic unit is not executable: it must be *instantiated* (section 14.2) to form an executable subprogram or package.

Each program unit is represented in the program text in two parts:

a **specification** and a **body**. The specification contains all the information about the unit that is visible from outside it; the body defines its execution. The specification is generally presented as the declaration of the unit (syntactically this is just the specification terminated by a semicolon); the body is presented separately as a declaration in its own right.

Program unit specifications and bodies may be nested in the bodies of other program units, and in block statements. Program unit specifications, but not bodies, may also be nested in package specifications.

The general rule of separate specification and body has the following exceptions.

(1) A package (or generic package) need not have a body. When necessary, in such a case, an empty body is assumed.

(2) A subprogram (but not a generic subprogram) need not have a separate specification. In such a case the body acts as the subprogram declaration.

(3) A subprogram may have a body written in another language (see pragma `INTERFACE`, section 12.5).

The code address of the body of a nongeneric program unit `P` is returned as a value of type `SYSTEM.ADDRESS` by the attribute

```
P'ADDRESS
```

The body of a program unit is an example of a **frame**: a construct which acts as the framework for declarations, statements, and exception handlers. The other kind of frame is the *block statement* (section 8.6). A frame has the general form

```
heading
   declarative_item;
   ...;
begin
   statement;
   ...;
exception
   exception_handler;
   ...;
end [name];
```

2 Lexical Structure

This chapter describes the basic elements of Ada source text: *characters* and *lexical elements*.

2.1 Character set

At the lowest level, Ada source text is a sequence of **characters** from the seven-bit coded character set of the International Standards Organisation (ISO standard 646). This contains 128 characters, numbered from 0 to 127, classified as **graphic characters** (32 to 126 inclusive, with graphical representations) and control characters (the rest).

For the purpose of Ada, the characters are further categorised:

(1) **Upper case letters**: `A B C ... Z`
(2) **Digits**: `0 1 2 ... 9`
(3) **Special characters**: `" & ' ( ) * + , - . / : ; < = > _ |`
(4) **The space character**
(5) **Format effectors**:

ht (horizontal tabulation)
vt (vertical tabulation)
cr (carriage return)
lf (line feed)
ff (form feed)

(6) **Lower case letters**: `a b c ... z`
(7) Other graphic characters
(8) Other nongraphic characters

Categories (1) to (5) contain the basic characters; they suffice to write any Ada program. The lower case letters (6) are equivalent alternatives to the corresponding upper case letters (1), except in character and string literals (section 4.3.1), in which all 128 characters can be used and are distinct. Categories (7) and (8) do not otherwise appear in Ada programs, except possibly in comments and for certain allowed replacements:

! for |
: for # in based literals (section 5.1)
% for " in string literals not containing " (section 4.3.1).

The Reference Manual, and this book, use the American National Standards Institute's ASCII representations of graphical characters. Alternative national representations are available, e.g. £ for # in the U.K. variant; the representation used does not affect the meaning of the program in any way.

Table 1 Character set

<table>
<tr><td></td><td></td><td colspan="8">1st hex digit</td></tr>
<tr><td></td><td></td><td>0</td><td>1</td><td>2</td><td>3</td><td>4</td><td>5</td><td>6</td><td>7</td></tr>
<tr><td>2</td><td>0</td><td>nul</td><td>dle</td><td>sp</td><td>0</td><td>@</td><td>P</td><td>`</td><td>p</td></tr>
<tr><td>n</td><td>1</td><td>soh</td><td>dc1</td><td>!</td><td>1</td><td>A</td><td>Q</td><td>a</td><td>q</td></tr>
<tr><td>d</td><td>2</td><td>stx</td><td>dc2</td><td>"</td><td>2</td><td>B</td><td>R</td><td>b</td><td>r</td></tr>
<tr><td></td><td>3</td><td>etx</td><td>dc3</td><td>#</td><td>3</td><td>C</td><td>S</td><td>c</td><td>s</td></tr>
<tr><td>h</td><td>4</td><td>eot</td><td>dc4</td><td>$</td><td>4</td><td>D</td><td>T</td><td>d</td><td>t</td></tr>
<tr><td>e</td><td>5</td><td>enq</td><td>nak</td><td>%</td><td>5</td><td>E</td><td>U</td><td>e</td><td>u</td></tr>
<tr><td>x</td><td>6</td><td>ack</td><td>syn</td><td>&</td><td>6</td><td>F</td><td>V</td><td>f</td><td>v</td></tr>
<tr><td></td><td>7</td><td>bel</td><td>etb</td><td>'</td><td>7</td><td>G</td><td>W</td><td>g</td><td>w</td></tr>
<tr><td>d</td><td>8</td><td>bs</td><td>can</td><td>(</td><td>8</td><td>H</td><td>X</td><td>h</td><td>x</td></tr>
<tr><td>i</td><td>9</td><td>ht</td><td>em</td><td>)</td><td>9</td><td>I</td><td>Y</td><td>i</td><td>y</td></tr>
<tr><td>g</td><td>A</td><td>lf</td><td>sub</td><td>*</td><td>:</td><td>J</td><td>Z</td><td>j</td><td>z</td></tr>
<tr><td>i</td><td>B</td><td>vt</td><td>esc</td><td>+</td><td>;</td><td>K</td><td>[</td><td>k</td><td>{</td></tr>
<tr><td>t</td><td>C</td><td>ff</td><td>fs</td><td>,</td><td><</td><td>L</td><td>\</td><td>l</td><td>|</td></tr>
<tr><td></td><td>D</td><td>cr</td><td>gs</td><td>-</td><td>=</td><td>M</td><td>]</td><td>m</td><td>}</td></tr>
<tr><td></td><td>E</td><td>so</td><td>rs</td><td>.</td><td>></td><td>N</td><td>^</td><td>n</td><td>~</td></tr>
<tr><td></td><td>F</td><td>si</td><td>us</td><td>/</td><td>?</td><td>O</td><td>ul</td><td>o</td><td>del</td></tr>
</table>

Note: *sp* = space, *ul* = underline

2.2 Lexical Elements

At the level above characters, Ada source text is a sequence of *lexical elements* and *separators*. **Lexical elements** are are the smallest meaningful elements of the language: *identifiers, literals, delimiters,* and *comments.* **Separators** are used to separate adjacent lexical elements: any number of separators is allowed between adjacent lexical elements (and before the first and after the last), and at least one must appear between adjacent identifiers and/or numeric literals. No separator is allowed within a lexical element. Separators are

- the space character (except in a comment, character literal, or string literal)
- any format effector (except `ht` within a comment)
- **end of line** (a format effector other than `ht`, and possibly some other implementation-dependent, non-character representation)

Note that a lexical element must fit on one line; this limits the length of identifiers, literals, and comments.

Identifiers are used as names. An identifier has the form

letter { [underline] letter_or_digit }

All the characters are significant, including the underlines, but upper and lower case letters are equivalent. Thus `A_1` is the same as `a_1` but different to `A1`.

The 63 **reserved words** (Table 2) are classified as identifiers, but are not available for general use.

Delimiters are the lexical elements, composed of 1 or 2 special characters, with fixed syntactic uses (see Table 2).

Literals represent values of certain types and are of 3 kinds: *numeric* (section 5.1) for integer and real values, *character* (section 4.3) for character values, and *string* (section 4.3.1) for one-dimensional arrays of character values.

2.3 Comments

A **comment** is a sequence of graphic, space, or *ht* characters, beginning with `--` and terminated by end of line. Comments are intended to guide the human reader, and do not affect the legality or meaning of the program. Multiline comments are written by repeating the `--` on each line:

```
I  := I + 1;   -- increment I

--  The above is an example of the sort of
--  thing that gives comments a bad name.
```

Table 2 Reserved words and delimiters

Reserved words:

abort	**else**	**mod**	**renames**
abs	**elsif**		**return**
accept	**end**	**new**	**reverse**
access	**entry**	**not**	
all	**exception**	**null**	**select**
and	**exit**		**separate**
array		**of**	**subtype**
at	**for**	**or**	
	function	**others**	**task**
begin		**out**	**terminate**
body	**generic**		**then**
	goto	**package**	**type**
case		**pragma**	
constant	**if**	**private**	**use**
	in	**procedure**	
declare	**is**		**when**
delay		**raise**	**while**
delta	**limited**	**range**	**with**
digits	**loop**	**record**	
do		**rem**	**xor**

Simple delimiters:

& ' ( ) * + , - . / : ; < = > |

Compound delimiters:

=> .. ** := /= >= <= << >> <>

Other characters used to form lexical elements:

" (or %)	in string literals (section 4.3.1)
# (or :)	in based numeric literals (section 5.1)
_	in identifiers (section 2.2) and numeric literals (section 5.1)
E (or e)	in numeric literals (section 5.1)
--	in comments (section 2.3)

3 Declarations, Types and Objects

3.1 Declarations and declarative parts

Declarations define entities of various kinds, and usually give them names. Some declarations are implicit in the presence of other constructs (see Table 5). Others are explicit; these are classified as **basic declarations** (see Table 3), and **non-basic declarations** (see Table 4). The distinction between declarations and specifications is purely syntactic: declarations are terminated by semicolons and specifications are not. Non-basic declarations always occur as parts of basic declarations. The Reference Manual also considers basic operations (see Table 6) to be implicitly declared.

Declarations are **elaborated** during execution of the program: the elaboration generally defines the declared entity and associates a name (an identifier, a character literal, or an operator symbol) with it. Until the declaration is elaborated the scope rules (section 3.2.1) ensure that the declared entity cannot be referred to. Exceptions may be raised during elaboration as during execution of statements – see section 9.1.

This chapter is concerned with declarations in general and with certain entities (types, subtypes, and objects) defined by them.

3.1.1 Basic declarations and declarative parts

Basic declarations occur in *package specifications* (section 11.1) and in the declarative parts of *frames* (section 1.10), with other declarative items (see Table 3). Only **basic declarative items** are allowed in a package specification. The order of declarative items in a declarative part must follow these rules:

(1) all *basic* declarative items must precede all *later* declarative items; declarative items which are basic or later may appear anywhere.

(2) if a program unit specification appears in a declarative part, then the corresponding body (if there is one) must appear later in the same declarative part.

Table 3 Basic declarations and other declarative items

declarative item	entity declared/effect	section
basic declarative items – basic declarations:		
object declaration	object (variable or constant)	3.4.1
number declaration	numeric constant	3.4.2
deferred constant declaration	constant of private type	11.4
type declaration	type	3.3.1
subtype declaration	subtype	3.3.2
exception declaration	exception	9.3
renaming declaration	additional name for an entity	3.2.5
basic declarative items – other declarative items:		
representation clause	specifies mapping on target machine	1.6
later declarative items:		
package body	body of package	11.2
subprogram body	body of subprogram	12.1.2
task body	body of task unit	13.1
body stub	stands for separately compiled body	10.2
basic or later declarative items – basic declarations:		
subprogram declaration	subprogram	12.1.1
package declaration	package	11.1
task declaration	single task or task type	13.1
generic declaration	generic unit (package or subprogram)	14.1
generic instantiation	package or subprogram	14.2
basic or later declarative items – other declarative items:		
use clause	allows direct visibility	3.2.4

Table 4 Non-basic declarations

declaration	entity declared	surrounding basic declaration	section
discriminant specification	discriminant of record type	record type declaration	6.2.3
		private type declaration	11.3
		incomplete type declaration	6.3.2
		generic parameter declaration	14.3
component declaration	component (not discriminant) of record type	record type declaration	6.2
entry declaration	entry or entry family	task declaration	13.1
parameter specification	formal parameter of subprogram	subprogram declaration	12.1.1
		generic subprogram declaration	14.1
		renaming declaration (for subprogram)	3.2.5
		generic formal subprogram declaration	14.3
		entry declaration	13.1.1
generic parameter declaration	generic parameter	generic declaration	14.1
enumeration literal specification	enumeration literal	enumeration type declaration	4.2
loop parameter specification	loop parameter	loop statement	8.5

Table 5 Implicit declarations

<table>
<tr><th>construct</th><th>entity declared</th><th>place of implicit declaration</th><th>section</th></tr>
<tr><td>named block statement</td><td>named block</td><td rowspan="3">end of declarative part of innermost enclosing frame</td><td>8.6</td></tr>
<tr><td>named loop statement</td><td>named loop</td><td>8.5</td></tr>
<tr><td>statement label</td><td>labelled statement</td><td>8.7</td></tr>
<tr><td>derived type declaration</td><td>derived operations</td><td>just after the derived type declaration (subprograms last)</td><td>3.3.3</td></tr>
<tr><td>type declaration</td><td>predefined operator</td><td>just after type declaration</td><td>7.1</td></tr>
</table>

Table 6 Basic operations

basic operation	example	associated type	section
assignment (and initialisation)	`V:=E;`	any nonlimited	8.2
allocator	**new** `T`	any type designated by an access type	6.3.6
selected component	`R.C, A.`**all**	record or access type	6.2.8
indexed component	`A(I, ...)`	array type	6.1.3
slice	`A(L..U)`	array type	6.1.3
qualification	`T'(E)`	any type	3.3.5
type conversion	`T(E)`	any type	3.3.4
numeric literal	`10,3.6e2`	*universal_integer, universal_real*	5.1
string literal	`"String"`	one-dimensional array of character type	4.3.1
null access value	**null**	any access type	6.3
record aggregate	`(C=>1,...)`	any record type	6.2.7
array aggregate	`(1,2,3)`	any array	6.1.4
attribute	`P'A,P'A(X)`	various	1.4

3.2 Scope and visibility

Every declaration has an associated **scope**, i.e. the part of the program text in which the declared entity can, in general, be referred to. Within the scope, at certain places defined by the *visibility* and the *overloading* rules, the name (identifier, character literal, or operator symbol) introduced by the declaration can be used to refer to the entity. In some cases the scope is two parts: the **immediate scope** where the name can be used alone, and an **extension** to the end of the scope of the enclosing declaration, where the name can be used in certain special cases (see below).

3.2.1 Scope

The scope of a basic declaration depends on the innermost declarative part or package specification in which it occurs, as shown in table 7. The scope always starts at the beginning of the declaration. In all cases, if a scope includes a body stub, it also includes the corresponding subunits.

The scope of an implicit declaration is defined in the same way; the place of the implicit declaration is shown in Table 5.

The scopes of declarations which form parts of other declarations are shown in Table 8.

Table 7 Scopes of basic declarations

place	immediate scope	extension
declarative part of frame	rest of frame	no
private part of package specification	rest of package specification plus body	no
visible part of package specification	rest of package specification plus body	yes, to rest of scope of package declaration

Table 8 Scopes of embedded declarations

declaration	enclosing declaration	immediate scope	extension
discriminant specification	private or incomplete type declaration	rest of enclosing declaration plus full type declaration and any representation clause for the type	no
discriminant specification	generic private type declaration	rest of enclosing declaration plus generic body	yes
discriminant specification or component declaration	record type declaration	rest of enclosing declaration plus any representation clause for the type	no
entry declaration	task declaration	rest of enclosing declaration plus task body	yes
parameter specification	subprogram declaration	rest of enclosing declaration plus subprogram body	yes
parameter specification	generic subprogram declaration	rest of enclosing declaration plus generic subprogram body	yes
parameter specification	entry declaration	rest of enclosing declaration plus all corresponding accept statements	yes
parameter specification	generic formal subprogram	rest of enclosing declaration	yes

Table 8 (continued) Scopes of embedded declarations

declaration	enclosing declaration	immediate scope	extension
parameter specification	renaming declaration	rest of enclosing declaration	yes
generic parameter declaration	generic declaration	rest of enclosing declaration	yes
enumeration literal specification	enumeration type declaration	rest of scope of enumeration type declaration	no
loop parameter specification	loop statement	rest of loop statement	no

3.2.2 Visibility

The visibility and overloading rules determine the meaning of an occurrence of a name. The visibility rules determine which declarations of the name are *visible* from the occurrence, and therefore possibly define its meaning. If there is no visible declaration, the occurrence is illegal. If there is just one visible declaration, that then defines the meaning of the name. If there are two or more visible declarations, the overloading rules apply, taking the context of the occurrence into account. Either they determine one of the visible declarations as defining the meaning of the name; or they fail and the occurrence is illegal.

The visibility rules are as follows.

(1) A declaration is not visible outside its scope, nor within itself except for a package declaration.

(2) A declaration is *directly visible* throughout its immediate scope, and as effected by a *use clause* (section 3.2.4), except where the declaration is *hidden* by a homograph (see below).

(3) A declaration is visible *by selection* in certain expanded names, selected components, and associations, where the prefix identifies the declaration (see Table 9).

(4) If D1 and D2 are two declarations of the same name, then D1 *hides* D2 in the following cases.

- D1 is a **homograph** of D2, i.e. they cannot be distinguished by the overloading rules (see below); and D1 occurs within a package specification, declarative part, or enclosing declaration (as in Table 5) within the scope of D2. D1 hides D2 throughout the immediate scope of D1, for direct visibility only.
- D1 is a homograph of the implicit declaration D2, in the same declarative part, or package specification plus declarative part of the package body. D1 hides D2 throughout its scope, for direct and by-selection visibility.
- D2 is any declaration; D1 is a subprogram specification, a generic subprogram instantiation, an entry declaration, or the formal part of an accept statement. D1 hides D2 throughout D1, for direct and by-selection visibility.

Table 9 Visibility by selection

declaration	place X of visibility by selection
any declaration in visible part of specification of package P	expanded name P.X
entry declaration in task type	expanded name T.X
component declaration or discriminant specification of record type	selected component T.X; named association X=>E in record aggregate or discriminant constraint
parameter specification in subprogram or entry declaration	named parameter association X=>E in subprogram or entry call
generic parameter declaration	named association X=>E in generic instantiation

3.2.3 *Overloading resolution*

Overloading resolution determines which of several visible declarations defines the meaning of an occurrence of a name. Only the following (impicit or explicit) declarations can be overloaded:

(1) a subprogram declaration (including an operation),
(2) an enumeration literal specification; this is treated as the declaration of a parameterless function delivering a result of the enumeration type,
(3) an entry declaration; this is treated as a procedure declaration with the same formal parameters.

The overloading is resolved on the basis of the number, types, and names of the formal parameters, and the result type for a function, as far as can be determined at the point of occurrence. The rules as to what information is taken into account are complex; it includes the number, types, and names (if given) of actual parameters in a subprogram or entry call, and the required type for a function call or enumeration literal. See the Reference Manual (section 8.7) for full information. Problems can usually be overcome by giving the compiler more information, e.g. by using named parameter associations or qualified expressions.

3.2.4 *Use clauses*

A **use clause** makes the declarations in a package specification directly visible. It has the form

```
use P, ... ;
```

where the `P` are the names of packages.

A use clause can appear in the context clause of a compilation unit (section 10.3), or in a package specification or declarative part of a frame. In the former case the effect of the use clause extends from the end of the use clause to the end of the compilation unit, and if the compilation unit is a specification, throughout its body. In the latter case the effect extends from the end of the use clause to the end of the package body or frame.

Every declaration in the visible parts of the packages `P` is made directly visible, unless hidden by a homograph, or if there are more than one such declaration with the same identifier, not all overloadable.

3.2.5 Renaming Declarations

A **renaming declaration** defines an aditional name J for an entity I; no new entity is defined. There are 5 forms, with particular rules.

```
J : T renames I;                                          -- (1)

J : exception renames I;                                  -- (2)

package J renames I;                                      -- (3)

procedure J [formal_part] renames I;                      -- (4)

function J [formal_part] return T
  renames I;                                              -- (5)
```

(1) I must denote an object of the base type of the type mark T; this may be a component of a composite object. If T is a constrained subtype, the constraints are ignored and the subtype of the object I is unaffected. If I is a record component that depends on a discriminant, then the record must be constrained. J must be an identifier.

(2) I must denote an exception. J must be an identifier.

(3) I must denote a package. J must be an identifier.

(4) I must denote a procedure or task entry (single or family member, but not an entry family) with the same number of parameters, and corresponding parameters having the same mode and base type, as in the formal part. J must be an identifier.

Any constraints implied by the formal part in the renaming declaration are ignored: the subtypes of the parameters are as for I. However the formal parameter identifiers and default expressions can be different for J than for I. A call to J is always a procedure call, not an entry call, even if I is a task entry (i.e. a call to J cannot be used in a conditional or timed entry call, and J'COUNT is illegal.

(5) I must denote a function with the same number of parameters, the same result base type, and corresponding parameters having the same mode and base type, as in the formal part. I and J must be identifiers or operator symbols, in any combination.

Any constraints implied by the formal part or result typemark T in the renaming declaration are ignored; the subtypes of the parameters and result are as for I. However the formal parameter identifiers and default expressions can be different for J than for I.

3.3 Types and subtypes

3.3.1 Types

A **type** is a set of values, and has an associated set of operations. Values of different types are distinct, and generally incompatible; thus a value of one type cannot (without *type conversion*, see section 3.3.4) be assigned to a variable of a different type.

Types fall into a number of different classes, see Table 10. For some classes there are predefined types provided by the language. A new type can be defined by a *derived type declaration* (section 3.3.3), by an *array object declaration* (section 6.1.2), or by an explicit type declaration for an enumeration, array, record or access type.

Table 10 Types and subtypes

class of type	constraints	predefined types	section
scalar – discrete:			
enumeration	range	CHARACTER, BOOLEAN	4.2
integer	range	INTEGER etc., *universal_integer*	5.2
scalar – real:			
floating point	floating accuracy, range	FLOAT etc., *universal_real*	5.4
fixed point	fixed accuracy, range	anonymous type(s), DURATION, *universal_fixed*	5.5
composite:			
array	index	STRING	6.1
record	discriminant	none	6.2
other:			
access	index, discriminant	none	6.3
task	none	none	13.1

Certain types are **limited.** For these, no assignment or equality and inequality operators are available. Limited types are:

- *task types* (section 13.1)
- *limited private types* (section 11.3)
- types derived from limited types
- array and record types with limited subcomponent types.

A **type declaration** has the basic form

```
type T is type_definition;
```

where T is an identifier. Record and task types have variations on this. Different classes of type declaration are described later in this chapter. Some of them (numeric, constrained array, and derived type declarations) in fact define an anonymous type and a subtype named T (called the **first named subtype**) of the anonymous type, rather than a type named T.

3.3.2 Subtypes

A **subtype** is a subset of a type (its **base type**), with the same set of operations; it is either the whole type (an **unconstrained subtype**), or else a subset defined by a **constraint** (a **constrained subtype**). A type is thus the same as its unconstrained subtype, and the terms are interchangeable, though for clarity the phrase *type or subtype* is often used. On the other hand, a constrained subtype is always regarded as different from its base type, even if it contains all the same values.

Objects and values of different subtypes of the same base type are compatible, though checks are made (leading to CONSTRAINT_ERROR if they fail) that values belong to the appropriate subtypes. An explicit test that a value belongs to a subtype can be made by using a *membership test* (section 4.1.4).

There are two predefined subtypes, both of the predefined type INTEGER: NATURAL and POSITIVE; see section 5.2.1. Other subtypes are defined, explicitly or implicitly, by subtype declarations.

A **subtype declaration** has one of the forms

```
subtype S is T;

subtype S is T constraint;
```

where S is an identifier and T is a **type mark**, i.e. the identifier of a type or subtype. S is defined as a subtype of the base type of T. If there is no constraint, S contains all the values of T and is in effect merely another name for T; S is unconstrained if T is a type or unconstrained subtype, and constrained if T is a constrained subtype. If there is a constraint, S is a constrained subtype containing the values of the base type of T that satisfy the constraint.

The classes of types and applicable constraints are shown in Table 10. The particular constraint is checked for compatability with any constraints applying to T; CONSTRAINT_ERROR is raised if the check fails.

A type mark optionally followed by a constraint

T [constraint]

is called a **subtype indication**; it is used in several places, besides subtype declarations, to specify a subtype as described above.

Elaborating a subtype declaration consists of elaborating the subtype indication, and then associating the identifier S with the resulting subtype. Elaborating a subtype indication without a constraint simply returns the subtype denoted by the type mark. Elaborating a subtype indication with a constraint consists of:

(1) evaluating the constraint.

(2) checking the value of the constraint for *compatibility* with the subtype T; CONSTRAINT_ERROR is raised if the check fails. **Compatibility** means in particular that any value of the base type of T satisfying the constraint is a member of the subtype T; additional rules are described in the section for each class of types.

(3) returning the subtype consisting of the values of the base type of T which satisfy the constraint.

3.3.3 Derived types

A **derived type** is a new distinct type which is a copy of another (parent) type, of the same class of types, with replicas of the parent type's values and operations. If the parent type is composite, the derived type has the same components with the same names, subtypes, and default expressions. If the parent type is a task type, the derived type has the same entries.

A derived type T is declared by a **derived type declaration**

```
type T is new S;
```

where `S` is a subtype indication. The subtype indication `S` is elaborated to define the **parent subtype**, and an anonymous type is defined which is a replica of the **parent type** (the base type of `S`), with a subtype which is a replica of the parent subtype. A set of derived operations for the derived type are also declared:

(1) the *basic operations* for the class of types (Table 6);
(2) *enumeration literals* for an enumeration type (section 4.2);
(3) the *predefined operators* for the class of types (section 7.1);
(4) *entries* for a task type (section 13.1.1);
(5) any **derivable subprograms** for the parent type. These are subprograms with a parameter or result of the parent type (changed to the derived mode in the derived subprogram) that are:

(a) declared in the same visible part of a package specification as the parent type (provided the derived type declaration is not in the same visible part), or

(b) derived subprograms of the parent type (itself a derived type), not hidden by any of (a).

A call to the derived subprogram is the same as a call to the derivable subprogram, with all actual parameters and result type converted (section 3.3.4): **`in`** and **`in out`** parameters converted to the parent type before the call, **`in out`** and **`out`** parameters and result converted to the derived mode after the call.

If a representation clause applies to the parent type, it applies also to the derived type, unless it is overridden by an explicit representation clause for the derived type. There may be particular restrictions on allowed representation clauses for a derived type, especially if it has derivable subprograms - check your User's Guide.

3.3.4 Type conversions

A **type conversion** causes a value to be explicitly converted to a given type. It has the form

```
T(E)
```

where `T` is the type mark of a type or subtype and `E` is an expression of the same or different type. `E` is evaluated, its value is converted to the base type of `T`, and the result is checked to belong to the subtype `T` (else

CONSTRAINT_ERROR is raised). If the target type has a different representation then the conversion includes a change of representation. The allowed type conversions are between the following pairs of types.

(1) Both types the same; or one derived from the other; or both derived from the same third type. In this case E must not be an allocator, an aggregate, a string literal, the literal access value **null**, or any of these in parentheses.

(2) Any two numeric types. Conversion to a real type is to within the accuracy of the subtype T (section 5.3). Conversion of real to integer is by rounding to the nearest integer (within the accuracy of the real subtype of E); rounding of exact halves is either way, undefined.

(3) Two array types with the same number of dimensions, corresponding index types convertible, and the same component type and subtype. If T is constrained, the components of E are checked to *match* (section 6.1.5) those of T (else CONSTRAINT_ERROR) and the bounds are those of T. If T is unconstrained, the bounds of the components of E are checked to belong to the index subtypes of T (unless E is a null array) else CONSTRAINT_ERROR is raised; and the bounds are those of E converted to the index subtypes of T.

The only implicit type conversions that take place are from *universal_integer* to an integer type, and from *universal_real* to a real type, when the operand is a numeric literal, named number, or attribute, and the target type is defined by the enclosing declaration, statement, or representation clause.

A value of any type may be converted to any other type, within any restrictions imposed by the implementation, by the use of **unchecked type conversion**. Instantiate the predefined generic function UNCHECKED_CONVERSION (section 14.2) with the source and target types, and call the instantiated function to do the conversion:

```
with UNCHECKED_CONVERSION;
...
V1 : T1; V2 : T2;
...
function T1_TO_T2 is
   new UNCHECKED_CONVERSION (SOURCE => T1,
                TARGET => T2);
...
T2 := T1_TO_T2(V1);
```

3.3.5 *Qualified expressions*

A **qualified expression** serves to define the type of an expression when it might otherwise be ambiguous, or to ensure that its value belongs to a particular subtype. It has the form

```
T'(E)
```

where `T` is a type mark and `E` is an expression of type `T'BASE`. If `E` is an aggregate only one pair of parentheses is needed:

```
T'(1,2,3)
```

The expression `E` is evaluated, and its value is checked to belong to the subtype `T` (else `CONSTRAINT_ERROR`).

3.3.6 *Attributes of types and subtypes*

The following attributes are defined for any type or subtype `T`.

attribute	type	value
`T'BASE`	(type)	base type of `T` (usable only as the prefix of a further attribute e.g. `T'BASE'LAST`)
`T'SIZE`	*universal_ integer*	the greatest number of bits that would be allocated to any object of (sub)type `T`

3.3.7 *Representation of types*

The following representation clause is available (if supported) for any type (or first named subtype) `T`. Other representation clauses for particular classes of types are described later.

```
for T'SIZE use E;
```

where `E` is a *static* expression (section 7.3) of an integer type. The effect is to allocate no more than `E` bits to objects of the type or subtype `T`. If `T` is a subtype, any constraints on `T` or its subcomponents (section 6.2.1) must also be static.

3.4 Objects

An **object** is an entity that contains a value of a particular type and subtype; every object has both a type and a subtype. A **variable** can hold different values (always of the same type and subtype) at different times; a **constant** always holds the same value.

Objects can also be created by *allocators* (section 6.3.6); *components* and *slices* of objects (sections 6.1.3, 6.2.8) are also objects. Other entities considered as objects are *loop parameters* (section 8.5), *formal parameters* (section 12.1.1), and *generic formal parameters* (section 14.1).

3.4.1 Object declarations

An **object declaration** has one of the forms

```
I,... : constant S := E; -- constant declaration

I,... : S [:= E];        -- variable declaration
```

For multiple declarations see section 1.8. `S` is a subtype indication specifying the type and subtype of the object. `E` is an expression of the same type.

If **`constant`** is present then the declared object is a *constant* with the value of the expression `E` (which must be present); otherwise the object is a *variable* , the expression `E` is optional and if present gives an initial value to the variable.

Access variables (section 6.3.4), *task variables* (section 13.1.2), and certain components of *record variables* (section 6.2.5) are implicitly initialised by default; in other cases without an initial expression the value of the variable is initially undefined. An attempt to evaluate a scalar object with an undefined value is erroneous; this applies to composite values only when scalar components are evaluated explicitly or predefined operators (which operate component by component) are applied.

Array object declarations may be combined with array type declarations - see section 6.1.2.

A single object declaration is elaborated as follows.

(1) The subtype indication `S` is elaborated, returning a subtype.

(2) If there is an initial expression `E`, it is evaluated; otherwise any default initial expressions (for components of a record type) are evaluated, in an undefined order.

(3) The object is created and any initial value is assigned to it. Initialisation is the same as *assignment* (section 8.2); in particular the same subtype checks are performed, and CONSTRAINT_ERROR is raised if they fail. Special rules apply for arrays, see section 6.1.2.

3.4.2 Number declarations

A special form of constant declaration for numerical objects is the **number declaration**:

```
I, ... : constant := E;
```

where the expression E is static and of type *universal_integer* or *universal_real* (sections 7.3, 7.4). For multiple declarations see section 1.8. This creates a **named number** I with the value and type of E, which can be used anywhere that the corresponding numeric literal (section 5.1) could be.

3.4.3 Attributes of objects

The following attributes are available for any variable or constant A, and perhaps also for named numbers.

attribute	type	value
A'SIZE	*universal_integer*	number of bits allocated to A
A'ADDRESS	SYSTEM.ADDRESS	address of first storage unit allocated to A

3.4.4 Representation of objects

The address of a declared object with identifier I (as returned by the ADDRESS attribute) can be specified by the representation clause (if supported):

```
for I use at E;
```

where E is an expression of type SYSTEM.ADDRESS.

4 Scalar and Discrete Types

Values of **scalar** types form ordered sets of individual values. Scalar types are **discrete** types and **real** types.

4.1 Discrete types

Discrete types are *enumeration* types, with values that are either characters of arbitrary values represented by identifiers, and *integer* types, with values that are (positive or negative) integers. Each value of a discrete type has a numbered **position** in the set. Besides their normal uses to declare objects, discrete types are of use as index types in constructing array types (section 6.1), and in controlling loop statements (section 8.5).

Integer types and real types are *numeric* types (section 5.3).

Every value of a discrete type has an **image**, its literal representation. This is the default for textual output (section 15.6) and can be accessed via the `IMAGE` attribute – see Table 11. On input, and for the `VALUE` attribute, any string having the appropriate lexical form is acceptable; this is

- for an enumeration value, the image, with any number of leading and/or trailing spaces
- for an integer value, an optional leading sign (+ or –) followed by any numeric literal form (section 5.1), with any number of leading and/or trailing spaces.

This always includes the image, so for any discrete value `X` of type `T`:

```
T'VALUE(T'IMAGE(X)) = X
```

4.1.1 Discrete subtypes

A subtype of a discrete type is formed by applying a **range constraint** to a discrete type mark `T` to give a subtype indication of the form

```
T range L .. U
```

where the bounds L and U are simple expressions (section 7.2), not necessarily static, of the base type of T.
The constraint is *compatible* (section 3.3.2) with the subtype T if each bound belongs to T. The subtype consists of all the values in the range. If the range is *null* (section 4.1.4), so is the subtype. The bounds L and U are evaluated in an undefined order.

Table 11 Images of discrete values

type	image
enumeration:	
graphic character C	character literal 'C'
nongraphic character	implementation-defined
other value L	identifier L
integer I:	
I = 0	" 0" (note leading space)
I /= 0	decimal literal, preceded by space (if I>0) or - (if I<0); no leading zeros, embedded underlines, or exponent

4.1.2 Discrete operations

The following binary operators are predefined for all discrete types, i.e. between two operands of the same discrete type.

(1) Equality and inequality: = /=
(2) Ordering operators: < <= > >=

Equality = and inequality /= have their usual meanings of identity of values and the converse; the relational operators refer to the implicit ordering for enumeration types, and have the usual arithmetic meanings for integer types. All results are of the predefined type BOOLEAN.

4.1.3 Attributes of discrete types

The attributes defined for a discrete type or subtype `T` are `T'BASE` and `T'SIZE` (section 3.3.6), and the following.

attribute	type	value
`T'FIRST`	`T'BASE`	lower bound of type or subtype `T`
`T'LAST`	`T'BASE`	upper bound of type or subtype `T`
`T'WIDTH`	*universal_ integer*	maximum length of the image of all values of `T`; 0 if `T` is a null subtype
`T'POS(X)`	*universal_ integer*	position number of `X` in type `T'BASE`
`T'VAL`	`T'BASE`	discrete value at position `I` in type `T'BASE`; `CONSTRAINT_ERROR` if `I` **not in** `T'POS(T'BASE'FIRST) .. T'POS(T'BASE'LAST)`
`T'SUCC(X)`	`T'BASE`	successor of `X` in type `T'BASE`: `T'POS(T'SUCC(X))=T'POS(X)+1`; `CONSTRAINT_ERROR` if `X=T'BASE'LAST`
`T'PRED(X)`	`T'BASE`	predecessor of `X` in type `T'BASE`: `T'POS(T'PRED(X))=T'POS(X)-1`; `CONSTRAINT_ERROR` if `X=T'BASE'FIRST`
`T'IMAGE(X)`	`STRING`	image of `X` in type `T'BASE`
`T'VALUE(S)`	`T'BASE`	value with literal representation `S` in type `T'BASE`; `CONSTRAINT_ERROR` if no such value

Notes

(1) `X` is an expression of type `T'BASE` (not necessarily in subtype `T`); `I` is an integer expression; `S` is an expression of type `STRING`.

(2) If `CONSTRAINT_ERROR` is not raised, then always:

- `T'POS(T'VAL(I)) = I, T'VAL(T'POS(X)) = X`
- `T'SUCC(T'PREC(X)) = X, T'PREC(T'SUCC(X)) = X`
- `T'VALUE(T'IMAGE(X)) = X`

4.1.4 Ranges

A **range** is a subset of a scalar type defined by two values of the type, the **lower** and **upper bounds**. It consists of all the values between the bounds, inclusive; i.e. if L and U are the lower and upper bounds respectively, the range contains all the values X for which (using the predefined ordering operators for the type)

```
L <= X and X <= U
```

If L > U then the range is a **null range** – it contains no values.

Ranges can be specified in several ways (see Table 12). The last two forms (involving T) are allowed only for discrete types; the first two are allowed for any scalar type. In the Reference Manual, the first two forms are called *ranges* ; all four forms (for a discrete type) are called *discrete ranges*.

A value can be tested for membership of a range (but not a discrete range of the last type) by a **membership test**:

```
E in R        -- TRUE if E is in range R

E not in R    -- TRUE if E is not in range R
```

where E is a simple expression (section 7.2) and R is a range. The result is of the predefined type BOOLEAN. The tests can also be used with the type mark of any constrained or unconstrained subtype in place of R. For real ranges the tests are subject to the usual accuracy limitations for real arithmetic (section 5.3).

Table 12 Ranges

range	lower bound	upper bound
`L .. U`	`L`	`U`
`A'RANGE [(N)]`	`A'FIRST [(N)]`	`A'LAST [(N)]`
`T`	`T'FIRST`	`T'LAST`
`T` **range** `L .. U`	`L`	`U`

Notes:

(1) T is the type mark of a discrete type or subtype; L and U are expressions (of type T in the last form); A is an array object, value, or (sub)type; N is a static integer expression.

(2) In a floating point constraint, L and U must be of real types.

4.2 Enumeration types

An **enumeration type** T is declared by a type declaration of the form

```
type T is (L, ...);
```

where the **enumeration literals** L are distinct identifiers or character literals (section 4.3). An enumeration type can contain all, some, or no character values; if it has one or more character values it is called a *character type* (see below). The enumeration values are ordered in the order in which they appear, with position numbers 0, 1, 2, ...

Each enumeration literal in the type declaration is an enumeration literal specification, and acts as a declaration of the enumeration literal. An enumeration literal specification L of type T is considered as equivalent to a function specification

```
function L return T;
```

where the function returns the enumeration value denoted by L.

The only operators and attributes defined for an enumeration type are those defined for any discrete type - see sections 4.1.2, 4.1.3.

4.2.1 Overloading of enumeration literals

An enumeration literal (character literal or identifier) can be *overloaded*, i.e. used in different enumeration types, representing distinct values. An overloaded enumeration literal can be legally used only when its type is determinable from the context; one way to ensure this is to *qualify* the literal `L` with its type `T`:

```
T'(L)
```

An enumeration literal which is an identifier can be overloaded by a parameterless function; resolution is by the *result type* of the function (see section 12.2.1). There are no parameterless operators to overload character literals. See section 3.2.3 for more information.

4.2.2 Representation of enumeration types

It is possible to prescribe the internal values to be used to represent the values of an enumeration type `T` by means of a representation clause

```
for T use (A,...);
```

where `(A,...)` is a *static* aggregate (section 7.3) of type **`array`** `(T)` **`of`** *universal_integer.* The prescribed values must retain the order of the enumeration values (though they need not be contiguous).

A subtype of an enumeration type is defined by applying a range constraint to the type mark of an enumeration type or subtype, as for any discrete type; see above.

4.3 Character Types

A **character type** is an enumeration type with one or more character values.

A character value if represented by a **character literal**: a single graphic character between apostrophes:

```
'A'  'a'  '('  '''  ' '
```

There is one predefined character type, `CHARACTER`, which contains all 128 characters of the ISO set, mapped on to the integers 0 to 127 (see Table 1). The graphic character values can be represented by character literals, if the characters are available on the program preparation medium. Alternative names for control characters, special characters, and lower case letters of type CHARACTER are provided by constant declarations in the predefined package STANDARD.ASCII (section 16.1.6).

4.3.1 String literals

String literals represent one-dimensional arrays of character values. A **string literal** is a sequence of 0 or more graphic characters (denoting the components, in order) enclosed in **string brackets**, which can be either " ", or (if the string contains no ") % %. In either case a string bracket character within the string is represented by two adjacent string bracket characters. Examples:

```
"This is a string."    ""    """%"""    %%%%
```

of lengths respectively 17, 0, 3, and 1.

The predefined type STRING is defined as packed unconstrained array of CHARACTER (section 16.1.8), but string literals are not confined to values of this type.

As a string literal cannot include control characters it is confined to one line. For a string value which is too long or contains control characters, use the *catenation operator* & (section 6.1.5) and if necessary the control names from package STANDARD.ASCII (section 16.1.6):

```
"This is a very long string, too long to " &
"fit on to one line." & ASCII.CR & ASCII.LF
```

4.4 Boolean types

There is one other predefined enumeration type:

```
type BOOLEAN is (FALSE, TRUE);
```

A **boolean type** is BOOLEAN or any type derived from it. BOOLEAN provides the result type for *relational operators* (section 7.1). Note that FALSE < TRUE.

4.4.1 Boolean operations

The following operators are available for boolean types.

(1) Equality and inequality: = /=
(2) Ordering operators: < <= > >=
(3) Logical operators: **and** **or** **xor** **not**
(4) Short-circuit control forms: **and then** **or else**

(1) and (2) are as for any *discrete type*, see section 4.1.2. (3) and (4) are defined in Table 13.

Table 13 Operations on boolean operands

operation	precedence	result type	operation
L **and** R	1	)	conjunction
L **or** R	1	) same	disjunction
L **xor** R	1	) as L	nonequivalence
L **and then** R	1	) and R	conditional conjunction
L **or else** R	1	)	conditional disjunction
not R	6	same as R	negation

Notes

(1) L and R are boolean operands of the same type.

(2) The logical operators are available also for one-dimensional *boolean arrays* (section 6.1.5).

(3) The short-circuit forms are not predefined operators, and cannot be overloaded. The other operations are predefined operators.

(4) The results are defined by the following truth table. T = TRUE, F = FALSE. (*) means that R is not evaluated.

L	R	L **and** R	L **or** R	L **xor** R	L **and then** R	L **or else** R	**not** R
T	T	T	T	F	T	T (*)	F
T	F	F	T	T	F	T (*)	T
F	T	F	T	T	F (*)	T	F
F	F	F	F	F	F (*)	F	T

5 Numeric Types

Numeric types are classified as *integer* and *real*, the former representing integers exactly and the latter representing real numbers approximately. Real types are divided into floating point types, with error bounds defined relatively, and fixed point types with error bounds defined absolutely.

There are predefined numeric types, from which all numeric types used in a program must ultimately derive. The predefined integer and floating point types are named (`INTEGER`, `FLOAT`, etc.) and so can be used directly, though this is usually inadvisable as they are implementation-dependent; the predefined fixed point types are anonymous. There are also the anonymous universal types known as *universal_integer*, *universal_real*, and *universal_fixed* , from which no further types can be derived (see section 7.4).

5.1 Numeric literals

Numeric literals represent integer and real values (of type *universal_integer* and *universal_real.* Real literals contain a decimal point, integer literals do not. Numeric literals are implicitly converted to other integer or real types as required by the context; but an integer literal is never converted implicitly to a real type or vice versa.

The most general form of numeric literal is a **based literal**, which specifies its base of notation explicitly:

```
R # S [. S] # [e X]
```

The **base** `R` (between 2 and 16 inclusive, unsigned) and the **exponent** `X` (representing multiplication by a power of the base, optionally signed) are in normal decimal notation. The exponent must not be negative (but may be zero) for an integer literal. The digit sequences `S` before and after the point are sequences of **extended digits** suitable to the base, i.e. from 0 to `R`-1 inclusive; letters `A` to `F` (or equivalently `a` to `f`) are used for 10 to 15. Leading zeros are allowed in the base, integer part, and exponent, and trailing zeros in the fractional part. In all parts successive digits may be interspersed with single underlines.

In case the character # is not available, both # may be replaced by colons. The letter e introducing the exponent may be in upper or lower case. Separators, including spaces, are not allowed within the literal.

If the base is 10 then a **decimal literal**, in which the base is implicit, can be (and usually is) used: this omits the base and the two #:

```
S [. S] [e X]
```

Examples of integer literals (all representing 42):

```
2#010_101_0#    7#6#e+1    42    16:002A:E0
```

Examples of real literals (all representing 14.25):

```
1.425e1    4#32.1#    10#0.14250_00#e+2
```

5.2 Integer types

5.2.1 Predefined Integer Types

An **integer** type or subtype consists of all the integer values between its lower and upper bounds, inclusive. There are one or more predefined integer types including (at least) the type `INTEGER`, and possibly others such as `SHORT_INTEGER` and `LONG_INTEGER`. These are meant to reflect the natural integer types of the target machine, i.e. the values representable in a word, halfword, or double word, etc.; their bounds `L` and `U` are implementation-dependent, but are symmetrical about 0 (except that an extra negative value is allowed): `L = -U` or `L = -U-1`.

There is also an anonymous predefined integer type known as *universal_integer.* It is not directly usable in the program; it is the type of integer literals and some other constructs - see section 7.4. It has at least the range of any other predefined integer type.

The position numbers of values of an integer type are the corresponding *universal_integer* values.

Two system values (of type *universal_integer*) are available in package `SYSTEM` (section 12.1.2): `SYSTEM.MIN_INT` and `SYSTEM.MAX_INT` are respectively the smallest and largest integers representable by any named predefined integer type.

5.2.2 Integer subtypes

As for any discrete type, a constrained subtype of an integer type is formed by the application of a *range constraint* to an integer type or subtype:

```
T range L .. U
```

The range constraint is *compatible* (section 3.3.2) with a constrained subtype T if all the values of the range belong to T. The subtype consists of the values in the range.

The bounds of the predefined types are implementation-dependent, so a range constraint that is compatible with a predefined type in one implementation may not be in another. An implementation-independent integer subtype can be declared by an **integer type declaration**:

```
type T is range L .. U;
```

where L and U are static integer expressions (not necessarily of the same type) giving the bounds. This declaration in fact defines an anonymous type *A* derived from one of the named predefined integer types P, chosen to accommodate all the values of the range, and defines a subtype T of *A* with the bounds L and U; it is equivalent to the declarations

```
type A is new P;
subtype T is A range A(L).. A(U);
```

If no named predefined integer type can accommodate the range, the declaration is illegal.

There are two predefined integer subtypes, for natural numbers including and excluding zero:

```
subtype NATURAL is INTEGER range 0 ..
  INTEGER'LAST;

subtype POSITIVE is INTEGER range 1 ..
  INTEGER'LAST;
```

5.2.3 Integer operations

The operations available for integer types are as follows.

(1) equality and inequality: = /=
(2) ordering: < <= > >=
(3) arithmetical: + - * / **mod** **rem** **abs**

(1) and (2) are the usual arithmetic operations. (3) are described in table 14. Mixed arithmetic with integer and real operands is possible; this is described under real types below.

Table 14 Operations on integer operands

operation	precedence	result type	operation
L + R	3	same as L and R	addition
L - R	3	same as L and R	subtraction
+ R	4	same as R	identity
- R	4	same as R	negation
L * R	5	same as L and R	multiplication
L / R	5	same as L and R	division
L **mod** R	5	same as L and R	modulus
L **rem** R	5	same as L and R	remainder
L ** N	6	same as L	exponentiation
abs R	6	same as R	absolute value

Notes

(1) L and R are of the same integer type. N is of type INTEGER.

(2) The operations of integer division L/R, modulus L **mod** R, and remainder L **rem** R are defined by the following relations (for R/=0, else NUMERIC_ERROR). See Table 15 below.

- L = (L/R)*R + (L **rem** R)
- sign (L **rem** R) = sign (L)
- **abs** (L **rem** R) < **abs** R
- L = R*N + (L **mod** R) for some integer N
- sign (L **mod** R) = sign (R)
- **abs** (L **mod** R) < **abs** R

(3) These operators are all predefined.

(4) Exponentiation is defined as follows; if N>0, L*L* ... *L (N factors); if N=0, 1; if N<0, NUMERIC_ERROR raised.

Table 15 Values of integer division, **mod**, and **rem**

L	R	L/R	L **rem** R	L **mod** R
+14	+3	+4	+2	+2
+14	-3	-4	+2	-1
-14	+3	-4	-2	+1
-14	-3	+4	-2	-2

5.3 Real types

Values of **real types** are finite approximations to real numbers. A real type or subtype is characterised by its range and its error bounds; it includes all the values within the range which can be represented within the error bounds (and possibly other values as well). There are two classes of real types according to the kind of approximation: *floating point types* with relative error bounds, and *fixed point types* with absolute error bounds.

Each real type or subtype has a set of numbers associated with it which are represented exactly: the **model numbers**. The model numbers are determined completely by the accuracy and range of the type or subtype, and the error bounds on calculations with real numbers are defined in terms of the model numbers. The model numbers are accessible to the program through attributes of the type or subtype (sections 5.4.5, 5.5.4). It is therefore possible, with care, to control the accuracy of calculations in an implementation-independent manner.

The interval between any two model numbers is called a **model interval**; this includes the case of a single model number. The result of any operation on real values is defined by consideration of the model intervals containing the operands: the result is defined only as falling within the smallest model interval containing all values that could result from applying the exact arithmetical operation to values in the smallest intervals containing the operands. This includes the *type conversion* of a real literal (section 3.3.4).

In general, the actual implementation can probably guarantee better error bounds than are defined by the model numbers. To allow full use of the underlying machine capabilities, a real type or subtype also has a set of **safe numbers**, which are also accessible to the program through attributes. These always include the model numbers, and actual error bounds on calculations are defined in terms of **safe intervals** in the same way as described for model intervals above. Reliance on safe numbers generally allows greater exploitation of the implementation, but yields less portable programs.

If the result of a real operation cannot be represented within the type (because of overflow), the exception NUMERIC_ERROR should be raised; however if this leads to great inefficiency the check may not be made. The attribute MACHINE_OVERFLOWS indicates whether the check is made or not for any particular real type.

5.3.1 Attributes of real types

The following attributes are available for any real type or subtype T.

attribute	type	value
bounds of type or subtype:		
T'FIRST	T	lower bound of (sub)type T
T'LAST	T	upper bound of (sub)type T
machine-dependent attributes:		
T'MACHINE_ROUNDS	BOOLEAN	TRUE if every predefined operation on values of type T'BASE is exact or rounds the result
T'MACHINE_OVERFLOWS	BOOLEAN	TRUE if every predefined operation on values of type T'BASE is correct (within the accuracy of the type) or raises NUMERIC_ERROR (i.e. overflow is always detected)

5.4 Floating point types

5.4.1 Predefined floating point types

There are one or more predefined floating point types including (at least) the type FLOAT and possibly others such as SHORT_FLOAT and LONG_FLOAT. These are meant to reflect the natural floating point types of the target machine.

The error bounds of a floating point type or subtype are specified by the number of decimal digits in the mantissa of the **decimal canonical**

form:

$$s\ m\ 10^e$$

where s is the sign (+1 or –1), m is the mantissa ($0 < m \leq 0.1$), and e is the decimal exponent (an integer). This number `D` is returned by the attribute `T'DIGITS` (see below), and in turn determines the number `B` of binary digits in the mantissa of the **binary canonical form**:

$$s\ m\ 2^e$$

where s = +1 or –1, $0 < m \leq 0.5$, and e is the binary exponent. In fact `B` is the smallest integer not less than `D` $\log_2 10 + 1$.

The *model numbers* have `B` digits in the binary mantissa, i.e. $m = n\ 2^{-B}$ where $0 \leq n \leq 2^{B-1}-1$. For a floating point type, the model numbers also have binary exponent in the range $-4\ B \leq e \leq 4\ B$; the coefficient 4 is chosen on pragmatic grounds.

The *safe numbers* of a floating point type have mantissae as model numbers but exponents e in an implementation-defined range `-E..E`, where `E >= B` (so the safe numbers include the model numbers).

5.4.2 Floating point subtypes

Subtypes of floating point types are defined by the application of **accuracy definitions** and/or **range constraints** to floating point types or subtypes:

```
T digits D

T range L .. U

T digits D range L .. U
```

Here `T` is a floating point type mark, `D` is a static simple expression of an integer type with a positive value, and `L` and `U` are expressions of type `T'BASE`. If no accuracy definition is given, the decimal accuracy `D` is the same as for `T`. If no range constraint is given, the range is the same as for `T` (within the error bounds of the subtype).

The constraint is *compatible* (section 3.3.2) with `T` if the bounds `L` and `U` of the range lie within the range of safe numbers of `T`, and the new decimal accuracy `D` is no greater than the decimal accuracy of `T`; if not, `CONSTRAINT_ERROR` is raised. Note that `L` and `U` need not be model numbers, or even safe numbers, of T; the requirement is for them to lie in the range defined by the smallest (most negative) and largest (most positive) safe numbers of T.

The model numbers of the subtype are defined from D as described for a floating point type above; they are a subset of the model numbers of the base type. They are not affected at all by a range constraint. The safe numbers of the subtype are just the safe numbers of the base type.

5.4.3 Floating point declarations

A floating point subtype can be declared in an implementation-independent way by means of a **floating point type declaration**, with one of the forms

```
type T is digits D;

type T is digits D range L .. U;
```

Here D is a static simple integer expression, with a positive value, defining the decimal accuracy required; this must not be larger than SYSTEM.MAX_DIGITS (section 16.2.2).

If a range constraint is supplied, the bounds L and U must be static simple expressions of some (possibly different) real types.

The floating point type declaration in fact declares an anonymous type *A* derived from one of the named predefined floating point types P, chosen so that its model numbers include the model numbers of T and the bounds L and U, if supplied, lie within its range of safe numbers; and then defines the subtype T of it with the given range and error bounds. It is equivalent to the declarations

```
type A is new P;
subtype T is A digits D;

type A is new P;
subtype T is A digits D range A(L)..A(U);
```

If there is no such predefined floating point type P, the program is illegal.

5.4.4 Floating point operations

The available operators for floating point types are as follows.

(1) equality and inequality: = /=
(2) ordering: < <= > >=
(3) arithmetic: + - * / ** **abs**

(1) and (2) are the usual numeric operators (subject to the considerations of error bounds described above); they yield results of the predefined type BOOLEAN. The arithmetic operations are described in Table 16.

Table 16 Operations on floating point types

operation	precedence	result type	operation
L + R	3	same as L and R	addition
L - R	3	same as L and R	subtraction
+ R	4	same as R	identity
- R	4	same as R	negation
L * R	5	same as L and R	multiplication
L / R	5	same as L and R	division
L ** N	6	same as L	exponentiation
abs R	6	same as R	absolute value

Notes

(1) L and R are operands of the same floating point type; N is of type INTEGER.

(2) Exponentiation L**N is allowed only with an integer exponent N, and is defined as follows: if N>0, L*L*...*L (N factors); if N=0, 1.0; if N>0, 1.0/(L ** -N).

(3) The operators are all predefined.

5.4.5 Attributes of floating point types

The following attributes of a floating point type or subtype T are defined, besides those defined for all real types (section 5.3.1).

attribute	type	value
properties of model numbers:		
T'DIGITS	*universal_ integer*	decimal accuracy D
T'MANTISSA	*universal_ integer*	binary accuracy B: $1 + D \log_2 10 \leq B < 2 + D \log_2 10$
T'EPSILON	*universal_ real*	length of smallest model interval just above 1.0: 2^{1-B}
T'EMAX	*universal_ integer*	largest binary exponent: 4B
T'SMALL	*universal_ real*	smallest positive model number: 2^{-4B-1}
T'LARGE	*universal_ real*	largest positive model number: $2^{4B} (1-2^{-B})$
properties of safe numbers:		
T'SAFE_EMAX	*universal_ integer*	largest binary exponent E (≥ T'BASE'EMAX)
T'SAFE_SMALL	*universal_ integer*	smallest positive safe number: (≤ T'BASE'SMALL)
T'SAFE_LARGE	*universal_ integer*	largest positive safe number: (≥ T'BASE'LARGE)
properties of the underlying machine representation:		
T'MACHINE_ RADIX	*universal_ integer*	radix R (number base of exponent)
T'MACHINE_ MANTISSA	*universal_ integer*	number of digits (for base R) in mantissa
T'MACHINE_EMAX	*universal_ integer*	largest (most positive) exponent (for base R)
T'MACHINE_EMIN	*universal_ integer*	smallest (most negative) exponent (for base R)

5.5 Fixed point types

5.5.1 Predefined fixed point types

There is a set of at least one predefined fixed point type; but unlike integer and floating point types, they are anonymous and cannot be used directly.

The error bounds of a fixed point type are defined by a value D, called the **delta** of the type. This determines another number d (called the **small** of the type); d is the largest power of 2 not greater than D, i.e. $d = 2^n \leq D$, $2^{n+1} > D$.

The *model numbers* of the type are 0 and all numbers having B digits in the mantissa m in the **binary canonical form**

s m d

where s is the sign (+1 or -1), m is the mantissa (a positive integer), and d is the small; i.e. $0 < m < 2^B$.

The *safe numbers* of a fixed point type are just its model numbers.

Two system values are available in package SYSTEM (section 16.2.2): SYSTEM.MAX_MANTISSA (*universal_integer*) is the largest possible number B of binary digits in the mantissa of a model number; SYSTEM.FINE_DELTA (*universal_real*) is the smallest possible delta D for a fixed point subtype with range -1.0 .. +1.0.

5.5.2 Fixed point subtypes

Subtypes of fixed point types are specified by the application of **accuracy definitions** and/or **range constraints** to fixed point types or subtypes:

```
subtype S is T delta D;

subtype S is T range L .. U;

subtype S is T delta D range L .. U;
```

Here D is a static simple integer expression; L and U are simple expressions of type T'BASE (not necessarily static).

The constraint is *compatible* (section 3.3.2) with T if the bounds L and U of the range belong to the range of safe numbers of T, and the new delta D is no greater than the delta of T.

As the predefined fixed point types are all anonymous, a fixed point type must be defined by a **fixed point type declaration** of the form

```
type T is delta D range L .. U;
```

Here D is a static simple expression of any real type, with a positive value defining the delta required. The bounds are static simple expressions of some (possibly different) real types.

The default value of the *small* d is defined as above, as the largest power of 2 not greater than D. However a representation clause is provided to override this: see below.

The range constraint limits the range of values in the usual way. It also determines the number B of binary digits in the mantissa of the model numbers: B is the smallest integer so that each of L and U is a model number, or differs from a model number by no more than d.

In fact the declaration defines an anonymous fixed point type *A* derived from one of the predefined fixed point types *P*, chosen so that its model numbers include the model numbers defined above, and a subtype T of that type; it is equivalent to

```
type A  is new P;
subtype T is A range A(L)..A(U);
```

5.5.3 *Fixed point operations*

The following operators are available for fixed point types.

(1)	equality and inequality:	=	/=			
(2)	ordering:	<	<=	>	>=	
(3)	arithmetic:	+	-	*	/	**abs**

(1) and (2) are the usual numeric operators (subject to the considerations of error bounds described above); they yield results of the predefined type BOOLEAN. (3) are described in Table 17.

Table 17 Operations on fixed point types

operation	precedence	result type	operation
L + R	3	same as L and R	addition
L - R	3	same as L and R	subtraction
+ R	4	same as R	identity
- R	4	same as R	negation
L * N	5	same as L	multiplication
N * R	5	same as R	multiplication
L * R	5	*universal_fixed*	multiplication
L / N	5	same as L	division
N / R	5	same as R	division
L / R	5	*universal_fixed*	division
abs R	6	same as R	absolute value

Notes

(1) Addition and subtraction are defined between fixed point operands L and R of the same type, giving a result of the same type.

(2) Multiplication and division are defined between one fixed point operand L or R and one INTEGER operand N, giving a result of the same fixed point type. Multiplication and division are also allowed between two fixed point operands L and R (not necessarily of the same type), giving an exact result of the special anonymous fixed point type *universal_fixed* which must be converted explicitly to a named numeric type. These latter operators are not predefined (they are declared in the environment package STANDARD, see section 16.1.4) and cannot be overloaded.

(4) There is no exponentiation operator.

5.5.4 Attributes of fixed point types

The following attributes of a fixed point type or subtype T are defined, besides those defined for all real types (section 5.3.1). The decimal representation assumed is that of a real decimal literal (section 5.1) with no underlines, exponent, or leading zeros, preceded by a space or -, and with just enough digits after the point to accommodate the decimal precision T'DELTA. If T'DELTA > 0.1, T'AFT = 1.

attribute	type	value
properties of model numbers:		
T'DELTA	*universal_real*	decimal accuracy or delta D
T'MANTISSA	*universal_ integer*	binary mantissa length B formodel numbers
T'SMALL	*universal_real*	smallest positive model number or small d
T'LARGE	*universal_real*	largest positive model number: (2^B-1) d
T'FORE	*universal_ integer*	length of integer part in decimal representation, excluding point (T'FORE ≥ 2)
T'AFT	*universal_ integer*	length of fractional part in decimal representation, excluding point ($-\log_{10}D \leq$ T'AFT $< 1-\log_{10}D$)
properties of safe numbers:		
T'SAFE_ SMALL	*universal_real*	smallest positive safe number: T'BASE'SMALL
T'SAFE_ LARGE	*universal_real*	largest positive safe number: T'BASE'LARGE

5.5.5 *Representation of fixed point types*

The *small* d of a fixed point type can be explicitly defined by a representation clause (if supported):

```
for T'SMALL use E;
```

where T is the type mark from the type declaration, and the value of the static simple expression E is real and not greater than the delta of the type. All subtypes of the type then have the value of E as *small*.

6 Composite and Access Types

A value of a **composite type** is made up of **components**, each a value of some type, possibly composite. Composite types are *array types*, in which the component types are all the same, and *record types*, in which they need not be. Constrained subtypes of composite types are defined by specifying certain values associated with the values of the type. Every value of a composite type with constrained subtypes belongs to one particular constrained subtype of the type.

A **subcomponent** of a composite value is a component of the value, or a component of a component of the value , and so on. No composite type `T` can have a subcomponent which has the same type `T`.

Values of an *access type* are pointers to objects of a particular type, created dynamically.

6.1 Arrays

6.1.1 Array types and subtypes

An **array** value is one or more dimensional array of component values, each of the same subtype (the **component subtype**), indexed in each dimension by a consecutive subset of the values of a discrete subtype (the **index subtype** for the dimension), not necessarily the same type or subtype for each dimension.

For the assignment of array values to array objects see section 8.2.

An **array type** includes all the array values with index ranges within the corresponding index subtypes, from null ranges at one extreme to the entire index subtype at the other.

There is one predefined array type: `STRING`, representing packed one-dimensional arrays of `CHARACTER` (section 4.3):

```
type STRING is array (POSITIVE range <>)
  of CHARACTER;
pragma PACK(STRING); -- see section 6.1.7
```

Constant `STRING` values may be represented by string literals - section 4.3.1.

Otherwise an array type A is defined by an **array type declaration:**

```
type A is array (T range <>, ...) of C;
```

where the type marks T identify discrete constrained or unconstrained subtypes, and the subtype indication C defines the subtype of the components. If C is an array or record subtype, it must be constrained.

A constrained array subtype S is defined by applying an **index constraint**, which specifies all the index ranges, to an array type or unconstrained subtype T;

```
T (R,...);
```

where the R's are *discrete ranges* (section 4.1.4) of the corresponding index subtypes, evaluated in an undefined order. The subtype contains just those array values of the base type in which the indexes of each dimension run through the full range R. If any range is null, then the subtype contains only **null arrays**, having no components; all such constrained subtypes are considered the same. Thus any array value belongs to just one constrained subtype.

The index constraint is *compatible* (section 3.3.2) with T if each discrete range R is contained in the corresponding index subtype of T; otherwise CONSTRAINT_ERROR is raised.

A constrained array subtype can also be declared thus:

```
type T is array (R,...) of C;
```

where the R's are discrete ranges. This form of array type declaration defines an anonymous array type *A*, with the discrete ranges R as its index subtypes, and defines the constrained array subtype T resulting from applying the index constraint to that type (i.e. the subtype containing all the array values with maximal numbers of elements). Thus it is equivalent to the declarations

```
subtype I is R1;   -- see below
...;               -- etc. for each index subtype
type A is array (I range <>, ...) of C;
subtype T is A (R,...);
```

where R1 is just R if R is a subtype indication, and T1 **range** R if R is a range with bounds of type T1.

If R is of the form L . . U then the types of L and U must be either:

(1) both *universal_integer*, in which case each of L and U must be an integer literal, a named integer number, or a *universal_integer* attribute. L and U are implicitly converted to type INTEGER
(2) both the same discrete type, which must be determinable, and must *not* be *universal_integer.*

It follows that if both L and U are overloaded enumeration literals, it may be necessary to qualify one: T'(L)..U or to use a subtype indication: T **range** L..U. Note also that this rules out

```
type T is array (-1..8) of C;
```

as -1 is not an integer literal and the type is not determinable (it could be *universal_integer* or INTEGER). Instead

```
type T is array (INTEGER range -1..8) of C;
```

or (better)

```
type I is range -1..8;
type T is array(I) of C;
```

can be used.

6.1.2 Array objects

An **array object** I can be declared by a normal object declaration (section 3.4.1), using a subtype indication S for a constrained array subtype

```
I, ... : [constant] S [:=E];
```

Here S is either the type mark of a constrained array subtype, or the type mark T of an unconstrained array subtype (i.e. an array type) followed by an index constraint as described above.

The initial value E is assigned to the declared object by the same rules as for an assignment statement (section 8.2); in particular, the bounds of the object are taken from the subtype, not from the initial value.

An array constant can also be declared using an *unconstrained* array subtype S:

```
I,... : constant S := E;
```

In this case the bounds of the constant are those of the value E.

Alternatively, an explicit array subtype can be avoided by a special declaration of the form

```
I,... : [constant] array (R,...) of C [:= E];
```

which declares one or more objects I of the corresponding constrained array subtype. The usual rules for multiple declarations apply (section 1.8). A single declaration of this form defines an anonymous array type *A*, and an anonymous constrained subtype *S* of *A*, formed by applying the index constraint (R,...) to the type *A*; and finally declares the object I. It is equivalent to the declarations

```
type S is array (R,...) of C;
I : [constant] S [:= E];
```

This is only the case of an anonymous subtype being defined in the language. Note that as a consequence of the interpretation of multiple declarations, every object declared in this way has a different type.

Array objects are always constrained. Unconstrained array types can be used for formal parameters (which are then constrained by the subtypes of the actual parameters) and function results.

6.1.3 Array components and slices

A component of an array object or value is accessed by an **indexed component**:

```
A(E,...)
```

where the prefix A is an array object name, a function call delivering an array, a slice of an array, or an array component of an array or a record; but not an array expression involving an operator. There is one expression E for each index position of the array, of the correct index type, giving the index values of the component.

A **slice** of a one-dimensional array object or value A is another array object or value of the same type consisting of 0 or more consecutive components of A:

```
A(R)
```

The prefix `A` is as for an indexed component; `R` is a discrete range with bounds of the index type of `A`.

The bounds of the slice are those of the discrete range `R`. Only one-dimensional arrays can be sliced, though a one-dimensional array of one-dimensional arrays can be sliced repeatedly:

```
type T is array (1..10) of C;
A : array (1..10) of T;
```

`A(2..4)(3..6)` is a slice of a slice.

The prefix `A` and the expressions `E` or the discrete range `R` are all evaluated in an undefined order. Checks are made at some point during the evaluation that the index values `E` or the bounds of `R` belong to the index subtype (except for a null slice); if a check fails `CONSTRAINT_ERROR` is raised.

6.1.4 Array aggregates

An **array aggregate** is an array value which explicitly gives the values of all components by means of named or positional associations `C` (section 1.7):

```
(C, ...)
```

A multidimensional array is treated as a one-dimensional array of arrays, i.e. the aggregates are nested, and the rules apply afresh to each nested aggregate. The only allowed array expression is for a subcomponent that is a one-dimensional character array, which can be represented by a string literal (section 4.3.1) (without catenation).

The usual rules of association apply (section 1.7), except that a mixture of named and positional associations is not allowed, and if there is only one component, it must be given in a named association (to distinguish it syntactically from an expression in parentheses). The names of components are expressions or discrete ranges of the appropriate index type, but a non-static expression or null range is allowed only if it is the only choice in the only association (in that dimension).

There are restrictions on array aggregates according to their context, deriving from the need to have defined bounds - see Table 18.

An array aggregate is evaluated by first evaluating all choices (including subaggregates) in undefined order, and then evaluating all expressions in undefined order. Checks are made at undefined points in the evaluation that all choices are in the corresponding index subtypes,

Table 18 Array aggregate bounds

others used?	named/pos. associations	bounds
aggregate is actual parameter, with formal parameter P		
yes	either	as P (must be constrained)
no	named	smallest . . largest choice value
no	positional	as P if constrained, else F..F+N
aggregate is generic actual parameter with generic formal parameter P		
yes	named	NOT ALLOWED
yes	positional	as P (must be constrained)
no	named	smallest . . largest choice value
no	positional	as P if constrained, else F..F+N
aggregate is return value from function returning type T, *or operand of qualified expression* T'A		
yes	either	as T (must be constrained)
no	named	smallest . . largest choice value
no	positional	as T if constrained, else F..F+N
aggregate is right-hand side of assignment V:=A		
yes	either	as type of V (must be constrained)
no	named	smallest . . largest choice value
no	positional	as type of V if constrained, else F..F+N
aggregate in any other context		
yes	either	NOT ALLOWED
no	named	smallest . . largest choice value
no	positional	F..F+N

Note: F is S'FIRST, where S is the index subtype. N is the number of components in the aggregate.

all expressions are in the component subtype, and all subaggregates have the same length; `CONSTRAINT_ERROR` is raised on failure.

The type of an array aggregate must be determinable from its context, without using any information from the aggregate itself. If the type is ambiguous, e.g. as actual parameter of an overloaded subprogram, it can be disambiguated by *qualification* (section 3.3.5):

```
T'(C,...)
```

6.1.5 Array operations

The following operators are predefined for array values, based on the predefined operators for the component types (see Table 19).

(1) equality and inequality = /= : for any number of dimensions and component type

(2) ordering relations < <= > >= : for one-dimensional arrays of discrete component type (**discrete arrays**)

(3) boolean operators **and** **or** **xor** : for one-dimensional arrays of *boolean* components (section 4.4)

(4) *catenation* & : for one-dimensional arrays of any component type.

Table 19 Operations on arrays

operation	prec	operand type	result type	operation
L **and** R	1	same 1-dimensional boolean array		conjunction
L **or** R	1	same 1-dimensional boolean array		disjunction
L **xor** R	1	same 1-dimensional boolean array		nonequivalence
L = R	2	any array	BOOLEAN	equality
L /= R	2	any array	BOOLEAN	inequality
L < R	2	discrete array	BOOLEAN	see below
L <= R	2	discrete array	BOOLEAN	see below
L > R	2	discrete array	BOOLEAN	see below
L >= R	2	discrete array	BOOLEAN	see below
L & R	3	any array or component type	same array type	catenation
not R	6	same 1-dimensional boolean array		negation

Notes

(1) Operations on 2 array values of the same type act on *matching*

components, i.e. components with the same index values, relative to the lower bounds.

(2) The logical operators **and**, **or**, and **xor** require operands of the same length; CONSTRAINT_ERROR is raised if this fails. They operate component by component, as does **not**.

(3) Two array values (of the same type) are equal if every component of each has a matching component of the other which is equal to it (using the predefined equality operator for the component type). All null array values of the same type are equal.

(4) Ordering of one-dimensional arrays is defined lexicographically. Matching array components are compared pair by pair, starting from the first, and using the predefined ordering relations for the component type, until one of the following happens:

- two unequal matching components are found: the array with the preceding component precedes the other array
- one array runs out of components before the other: the one that runs out precedes the other (a null array precedes any non-null array of the same type)
- the arrays run out simultaneously: the two arrays are equal.

(5) The **catenation operator** & applies to any one-dimensional array type and to two operands each of which is an array or a component; the result is the array resulting from appending the right operand to the left operand, with bounds as shown in Table 20.

Table 20 Catenation

L	R	L & R
array(L1..U1)	array(L2..U2)	array(L1..U1+U2-L1+1)
array(L1..U1)	C	array(L1..U1+1)
array(L1..U1)	null array	array(L1..U1)
C	array(L2..U2)	array(F..F+U2-L2+2)
C	C	array(F..F+2)
C	null array	array(F..F+1)
null array	array(L2..U2)	array(L2..U2)
null array	C	array(F..F+1)
null array	null array	null array

Note: array(L..U) means **array** (T **range** L..U) **of** C, with L <= U; and F = T'FIRST.

6.1.6 *Attributes of arrays*

The following attributes are defined for an array object, value, or constrained subtype A.

attribute	type	value
A'FIRST(N)	Nth index type	Nth lower bound
A'LAST(N)	Nth index type	Nth upper bound
A'RANGE(N)	(range of Nth index subtype)	A'FIRST(N)..A'LAST(N)
A'LENGTH(N)	*universal-integer*	length of Nth dimension: A'LAST(N)-A'FIRST(N)+1

Here N is a static universal integer expression, between 1 and the dimensionality of A inclusive; if N=1, the (N) can be omitted. A'RANGE can be used anywhere a range or discrete range is required, unless explicitly forbidden.

6.1.7 *Representation of arrays*

There are no special representation clauses for arrays. The representation of individual components can be affected by representation clauses on the component type. The layout of components within an array can be affected by the pragma PACK:

```
pragma PACK (A);
```

where A is the identifier from an array type declaration. The effect is to request the compiler to lay out values of the type A so as to reduce the wasted storage allocated between components. The pragma may appear anywhere that a representation clause for the type can. It does not apply to any types derived from A.

6.2 Records

6.2.1 Record types

A **record** value is a composite value containing 0 or more components, not restricted to be of the same type, and accessed by name. The components may be scalars, arrays, access values, tasks, or records.

A record type may have special components called *discriminants.* A record type without discriminants has the same components, of the same constrained subtypes, in all values of that type. A record type with one or more discriminants may have values with different components, or the same components but of different subtypes. Discriminants are discussed further below.

There are no predefined record types; a record type is declared by a **record type declaration**.

6.2.2 Record types without discriminants

A record type declaration without discriminants has one of the forms:

```
type T is                          type T is
  record                             record
    C;                                 null;
    ...;                             end record;
  end record;
```

The second form declares a *null record type,* with no components. In the first form each **component declaration** `C` has the form

```
I,... : S [:= E];
```

where the `I` are the component identifiers, `S` is a subtype indication, and `E` is an expression of the base type of `S`. The usual rules for multiple declarations apply (section 1.8).

Each subtype indication is elaborated, but the default expressions `E` are not evaluated yet. (They are evaluated if required when the record type is used to declare an object – section 6.2.5.)

The identifiers `I` of the components must all be different; they cannot be used within the subtype indications `S` and default expressions `E` of the components of the same record type declaration. Components of limited types (section 3.3.1) cannot have default expressions.

A record type without discriminants has no constrained subtypes, though it may be considered to be a constrained subtype of itself.

6.2.3 Discriminants and variant parts

A record type declaration with discriminants has one of the forms

```
type T (D;...) is            type T (D;...) is
  record                       record
    C;                           null;
    ...;                       end record;
  end record;
```

The **discriminants**, defined in the **discriminant part** `(D,...)`, are components with values on which the existence or properties of other components may depend. A **discriminant specification** `D` has the same form as a component declaration

```
I,... : S [:= E]
```

except that the subtype indication `S` may not have constraints, and default expressions `E` must be provided for all discriminants or none.

Note also that semicolon is used as a separator, not a terminator; there is no final semicolon. The usual rules for multiple declarations apply (section 1.8).

This form of record type declaration is elaborated as for a type without discriminants except that:

(1) the discriminant specifications are elaborated first, in order, before the component declarations; all this does is define the discriminants (the default expressions are not evaluated yet)

(2) if a component's subtype indication has a bound or discriminant value which is a discriminant (see below), that bound or discriminant value is left unevaluated. All other parts of component subtype indications are evaluated as usual.

Discriminants always have defined values, and there are restrictions on changing their values - see below.

A discriminant cannot be used within its discriminant part. It can be used to control other components (not discriminants) as follows:

(1) it can be used in a default expression

(2) it can be used (alone, not as part of an expression) as a bound in an index constraint (of an array or access component), or as a discriminant value in a discriminant constraint (of a record or access component), in a component's subtype indication

(3) it can be used to control a variant part (the type of such a discriminant cannot be a *generic formal type* – section 14.3).

A **variant part** appears as the final component declaration. It specifies alternative lists of components, depending on a discriminant value. It has a form like a case statement, and the same rules governing the values of the choices (there must be a choice for each value of the subtype of the discriminant if it is static, otherwise for each value of its base type; and no others: see section 8.4).

```
case D is
  when X:... =>
    C;
    ...;
  ...;
end case;
```

D is the identifier of the discriminant governing the variant part. The X are the choices defining the values of D for which the following components C exist. Possible forms of X are: a static simple expression, a static discrete range, and **others** on its own at the end. The rules of associations (section 1.7) apply; the set of values to be covered is the subtype of D if it is static, otherwise the type of D.

The component declarations C in the variant part are as defined above; in particular, although only one variant part is allowed in any record type, there can be a nested variant part (at the end) depending on the same or another discriminant. All the component identifiers, including those in all nested variant parts, must be different. An empty variant is allowed:

```
when X;... =>
  null;
```

6.2.4 Record subtypes

A constrained record subtype S is defined by applying a **discriminant constraint**, which specifies the values of all the discriminants, to a record type or unconstrained subtype T with discriminants:

```
T ([D|... =>] E,...)
```

The *discriminant associations* follow the rules of section 1.7, and provide one value for each discriminant D. Both named associations and positional associations are possible; the names D are the discriminant names, and the expressions E are of the discriminant types.

The subtype indication is elaborated by evaluating the expressions E in an undefined order (once for each discriminant in a named association). The constraint is *compatible* (section 3.3.2) with T if the value of each expression E is in the subtype of the discriminant D, and for each component subtype indication with a constraint containing a discriminant, the constraint is compatible with the type mark when the discriminant value is substituted. If either check fails, CONSTRAINT_ERROR is raised.

The subtype defined contains the record values of the type T with the values of the discriminants given by the expression E. Thus every record value with discriminants is of a particular constrained subtype, given by its discriminant values.

6.2.5 Record objects

A record variable is declared by a normal object declaration

```
I,... : S [:= E];
```

where S is a record subtype indication.

If the base type T of S has no discriminants, then the objects have all the components of T, with any initial values given by the initial expressions E of the object declaration, or failing that, the default initial expressions of T.

If the base type T has discriminants, then the subtype S may be unconstrained or constrained.

If T has discriminants and S is unconstrained, then T must have default initial expressions for its discriminants (else the program is illegal), and the object's discriminant values are taken from the default expressions of T. In this case the variable is **unconstrained**; the discriminants can have their values changed, but not individually - an assignment to the entire record value is needed.

If T has discriminants and S is constrained (by a discriminant constraint obeying the same rules as for a record subtype declaration), then the object's discriminants have the values from the constraint, and they are unchangeable; the variable is **constrained**. An assignment to the record object as a whole must not change the values of the discriminants; any such attempt raises CONSTRAINT_ERROR.

A record constant is declared by a normal constant declaration

```
I,... : constant S := E;
```

and is always constrained.

A record object can also be created by an *allocator* (section 6.3.6); such an object is always constrained. A formal parameter (section 12.1.1) of a record type is constrained if its subtype is constrained, the corresponding actual parameter is constrained, or its mode is **in**.

6.2.6 Values of discriminants

The values of discriminants are initially derived as follows.

(1) For a declared record variable (or record subcomponent of a declared record or array variable) of a constrained subtype: from the subtype.

(2) For a declared record variable or subcomponent of an unconstrained subtype: from the default expressions (which must exist) of the record type.

(3) For a declared record constant: from the initail value (which must be the same as in the discriminant constraint, if the subtype of the constant is constrained).

(4) For an allocated record object: from the allocator.

(5) For a formal parameter: from the actual parameter.

Discriminant components cannot be assigned values individually; they cannot be used as actual parameters of mode **out** or **in out**, or as generic actual parameters of mode **in out**. The only way in which the value of a discriminant can be changed is by assignment to the entire record object, and that is possible only if the subtype of the object is unconstrained (so that the initial values of its discriminants are taken from the default expressions of the base record type). The discriminant values of an allocated record object can never be changed.

6.2.7 Record aggregates

A **record aggregate** is a record value defined in terms of the values of its components. It has the form

```
([X|... =>] E,...)
```

where each expression `E` has the type of all the associated components `X`.

The *component associations* follow the usual rules (section 1.7) and provide one value for each component (including discriminants, which come first in position). The choices X are component names or **others**. Additional rules are as follows.

(1) If **others** appears it must represent one or more components (all of the same type).
(2) If there is only one component, it must be given by a named association (to distinguish it syntactically from an expression in parentheses).
(3) If there is a variant part, then the expression E for the discriminant X which governs it must be static, and the corresponding components in the variant part must appear.
(4) If a component value does not belong to the component subtype, CONSTRAINT_ERROR is raised.

The type of the aggregate must be determinable from the context; it can be disambiguated if necessary by qualification by the type T:

```
T'([X|... =>] E,...)
```

6.2.8 Selected components

A component of a record object or value is referred to by a **selected component**

```
R.C
```

where R is a name denoting a record object (possibly itself an indexed or selected component) or a function call delivering a record result, and C is the identifier of one of its components (including discriminants).
If C is a component in a variant part, CONSTRAINT_ERROR is raised if the discriminant values are such that C does not exist.

6.2.9 Record operations

The only predefined operators for record operands are equality = and inequality /=, defined for record values of the same type. and yielding a result of the predefined type BOOLEAN. Two record values are equal if they have equal values in all corresponding components, including discriminants. Assignment of entire records is possible – see section 8.2.

6.2.10 Attributes of records

The following attributes are associated with records.

attribute	type	value
for an object A of a record type with discriminants:		
A'CONSTRAINED	BOOLEAN	TRUE if A is constrained, i.e. is a constant or a variable with a constrained subtype; FALSE otherwise
for a component C (including discriminants) of a record type:		
C'POSITION	*universal_integer*	offset of component from start of record (in storage units)
C'FIRST_BIT	*universal_integer*	bit offset of first bit of component from first bit of C'POSITION storage unit
C'LAST_BIT	*universal_integer*	bit offset of last bit of component C from first bit of C'POSITION storage unit

6.2.11 Representation of records

The layout of the components of values of a record type can be affected by use of the pragma PACK:

```
pragma PACK(R);
```

where R is the identifier from a record type declaration. This requests the compiler to lay out values of type R so as to minimise the wasted store between components. The pragma may appear anywhere that a representation clause for type R can (section 1.6). It has no effect on types derived from R.

The storage representation of a record type T (and all its subtypes) can be accurately controlled by a *record representation clause.* This has the form

```
for T use
  record [at mod A;]
    [C at E range R;
     ...;]
  end record;
```

A and the E are static simple integer expression; the R are static integer ranges; and the C are component identifiers of the record type T.

The effect of the **alignment clause**

```
  at mod A;
```

is to force all objects of type T to start on an address that is a multiple of the value of A (usually a power of two). Allowable values of A are machine dependent.

The effect of a **component clause**

```
C at E range R;
```

is that component C is stored starting E storage units from the start of the record, in bit positions given by R relative to the first bit of that storage unit. E and R are returned by the attributes C'POSITION and C'FIRST_BIT..C'LAST_BIT. Component clauses may be given for none, some or all components (including discriminants), but no more than one for any one component. The component clauses must not cause components to overlap (except in different variants), and must allow enough room for every possible value of the component (as defined by its subtype, if static, or its type if not). A compiler may impose other restrictions or support other facilities - consult your User's Guide.

6.3 Access types

6.3.1 Access types and subtypes

Values of **access types** are pointers to objects which are created dynamically, during the execution of the program, and are accessible only via access values. Access values which point to, or *designate,* objects, and the objects themselves, are created by the evaluation of *allocators*; access values can only designate such allocated objects, not objects created by elaborating declarations. Values of an access type designate only objects of a particular type (the **designated type**).

Each access type also includes a special value **null** which designates no object and so is different to every other value of the type.

An access type A is declared by an **access type declaration**

```
type A is access S;
```

Here S is a subtype indication (section 3.3.2) of a constrained or unconstrained subtype called the **designated subtype** of A. The **designated type** of A is the base type of S. If the designated subtype is constrained, an access object of type A can be assigned only values designating objects satisfying the constraint (or CONSTRAINT_ERROR is raised); in effect A is a constrained access subtype.

6.3.2 Incomplete type declarations

Recursive definition of an access type is possible by means of an **incomplete type declaration**, with one of the forms:

```
type T;          or          type T(D;...);
```

This defines the identifier T to be the type mark of a type; the second form further defines T to be a record type with the discriminant part (D;...) – see section 6.2.3. The type mark T may then be used in an access type declaration of the form

```
type A is access T;
```

or, optionally for the second form, with a discriminant constraint

```
type A is access T([D|...] => E;...);
```

The type T must be fully defined by a *type declaration* (section 3.3) or (for the first form only) a *task type declaration* (section 13.1). For the second form, the full type declaration must declare a record type with a discriminant part that *conforms* (section 1.9) to that in the incomplete type declaration. For the first form T can be an unconstrained array or record type. Outside the scope of the full type declaration, the type mark T can be used only in access type declarations as shown above.

The position of the full or task type declaration is as follows.

incomplete type declaration:	full or task type declaration:
declarative part	later, in same declarative part
package specification, visible part	later, in same visible part
package specification, private part	later, in same private part or declarative part of package body

6.3.3 Subtypes of access types

A constrained subtype of an access type is defined by applying a constraint to the type mark of an access type:

```
A    constraint
```

where `A` is the type mark of an access type. The designated subtype of `A` must be unconstrained; the only constraints allowed are:

(1) an index constraint, if the designated type of `A` is an array type
(2) a discriminant constraint, if the designated type of `A` is a record type.

If the constraint is not *compatible* (section 3.3.2) with the designated type of `A`, `CONSTRAINT_ERROR` is raised. The values of the subtype are those that designate objects satisfying the constraint.

6.3.4 Access objects

An access object is declared by a normal object declaration

```
I, ... : [constant] S [:= E];
```

where `S` is a subtype indication for an access type or subtype. The usual rules for multiple declarations apply (section 1.8); in particular, if `E` is an allocator, a new allocated object is created for each declared object `I`. An access object can also be created by an allocator, as for an object of any type.

In the absence of explicit initialisation, initially any access value (whether created by a declaration or by an allocator) has the special value **null** which points nowhere. An attempt to access the designated object raises `CONSTRAINT_ERROR`.

6.3.5 Access to allocated objects

Access to an allocated object is always via an access value designating it. If A is a name of the access value, the designated object is referred to by the special form of **selected component**

```
A.all
```

If the designated object is an array or a recored, then its components can be accessed via the short forms

- *indexed component* of array (section 6.1.3):

  `A(I,...)` for `A.all(I,...)`

- *slice* of array (section 6.1.3):

  `A(R)` for `A.all(R)`

- *selected component* of record (section 6.2.8) or *task entry* (section 13.1.1):

  `A.C` for `A.all.C`

Similar short forms are available for certain attributes applying to designated objects. These are

(1) for an array object (section 6.1.6):

```
A'FIRST [(N)]   for A.all'FIRST [(N)]
A'LAST [(N)]    for A.all'LAST [(N)]
A'LENGTH [(N)]  for A.all'LENGTH [(N)]
A'RANGE [(N)]   for A.all'RANGE [(N)]
```

(2) for a task object (section 13.1.4):

```
A'TERMINATED    for A.all.TERMINATED
A'CALLABLE      for A.all.CALLABLE
```

`CONSTRAINT_ERROR` is raised in all these cases if A is **`null`**.

Other attributes of objects, `A'SIZE` and `A'ADDRESS` (section 3.4.3), apply to the access object `A`, not to the designated object.

6.3.6 *Allocators*

An **allocator** has one of the forms

```
new T [constraint]

new T'(E)
```

Here `T` is a type mark, the optional constraint is a discriminant constraint or an index constraint (in this case `T` must denote an appropriate record or array type, respectively), and `E` is an initial expression or an array or record aggregate (without the outer parentheses, i.e. only one outer pair is required).

Evaluation of an allocator causes the constraint to be elaborated, or the expression or aggregate `E` to be evaluated. An allocated object is then created, with an initial value given by `E` in the second case, otherwise implicitly by evaluating any default expressions in the type declaration for `T` or (for discriminants) from the discriminant constraint.

The value of the allocator is an access value designating that object, of an access type with the correct designated type, which must be unambiguously determinable from the context.

In each case the type of the allocated object is the base type of `T`. If the type is an array or record type with discriminants, the allocated object is constrained; values for the bounds or discriminants must be provided:

(1) in the first case witout a constraint, by the constrained subtype `T`, or (for a record type) by default values in the type declaration for `T`,
(2) in the first case with a constraint, by the constraint,
(3) in the second case, by the bounds or discriminants of the initial value `E`.

If the type is not an array or record type, the subtype of the created object is the designated subtype of the access type of the allocator.

6.3.7 *Access operations*

The only predefined operators for access operands are equality = and inequality /=. Two access values are equal if they are both **null** or designate the same object (not just objects with the same value).

6.3.8 *Attributes of access types*

The following attribute is defined for any access type or subtype T.

attribute	type	value
T'STORAGE_SIZE	*universal_integer*	number of storage units reserved for the collection of the base type of T

6.3.9 *Storage control*

All the objects designated by values of a particular access type (and all its derived types, section 3.3.3) form a **collection**. If an object in a collection has no access values designating it, then it is forever unreachable: in such cases some implementations recover the space for reuse (this is called *garbage collection)*, but as this can impose unforeseeable performance overheads it is not compulsory. However, when the scope of the declaration of the access type is left, the whole collection becomes unreachable, and implementations are expected to recover the space at that time. Check this in your User's Guide if it is important to your application.

Automatic garbage collection can be inhibited by use of the pragma

```
pragma CONTROLLED(A);
```

where A is the type mark for an access type (not a derived type). This pragma can appear in the same place as a representation clause for A (section 1.6); it stops automatic recovery of space for objects designated by values of type A, and any types derived from A, except on leaving the scope of the declaration of A.

Finer control over space recovery can be achieved by using **unchecked deallocation**: to do this, instantiate the generic procedure UNCHECKED_DEALLOCATION (section 16.2.3) with the object and access types as the generic actual parameters, and then call it with the access value as parameter:

```
with UNCHECKED_DEALLOCATION;
...
type T is ...;
type AT is access T;
TPTR : AT := new T;
procedure F is new UNCHECKED_DEALLOCATION
   (OBJECT => T, NAME => AT);
...
F(TPTR);
```

This has no effect if the access value is **null**, otherwise it recovers the space occupied by the allocated object and sets the value of the access object to **null**.

The amount of space reserved for a collection can be controlled by use of the representation clause

```
for T'STORAGE_SIZE use E;
```

where T is the access type, and the expressions E is of an integer type (not necessarily static), giving the value in storage units.

7 Expressions, Operands and Operators

7.1 Names

Names are used to denote entities of many kinds.

A *simple name* is an *identifier* (section 2.2), a *character literal* (denoting a character value – section 4.3), or an *operator symbol* (denoting an operator – 12.2). (In the Reference Manual, *simple name* is used only for identifiers and *compound name* is not used.)

A *compound name* is formed from the name of an entity (the **prefix**) to denote an entity associated with it. They are of two kinds.

(1) A *component* of an array (section 6.1.3) or a record (section 6.2.8), a *slice* of an array (section 6.1.3), an object *designated* by an access value (section 6.3), an *entry* of a task (section 13.1.1). Here the prefix may be a name (simple or compound) or a function call returning a result of an appropriate type.

(2) An entity declared in the visible part of a package specification (section 11.1); or an entity declared in a surrounding named construct (program unit, block, loop, or accept statement). In the latter case the name can be used only within the named construct. This form is called an *expanded name*, and has the same form as a selected component

```
P.I
```

where the prefix `P` is a name of the package or construct and `I` is the simple name of the entity. For an accept statement the corresponding single entry or entry family name is used as the prefix.

7.2 Expressions

Expressions allow values to be combined by the application of operators to form other values. This process is called **evaluation** of the expressions. The constituent values are represented by **operands**, which may be names, literals, aggregates, or various forms of subexpression (see Table 21). The order in which operands are evaluated and operators are applied is controlled by the precedences of the operators and the use of parentheses:

(1) the order of evaluation of the two operands of a binary operator is undefined

(2) operators at the same parenthesis level are evaluated in order of decreasing precedence (Table 22), and from left to right for operators of the same precedence. Thus `A+B-C+D` means `((A+B)-C)+D`; `A+B/C*D` means `A+((B/C)*D)`.

The different forms of operand are summarised in Table 21. The available operators are summarised in Table 22; they comprise:

(1) the membership tests **in** and **not in**, and the short-circuit control forms **and then** and **or else**, which are *basic operations* rather than operators

(2) the fixed point operators * and / yielding *universal_fixed* results; these are declared in package `STANDARD`

(3) the rest are the predefined operators; these are implicitly declared with the type declaration for each applicable type and can be redefined or have their definitions extended to new types by operator declarations (section 12.2.1).

In the operator declarations for (2) and (3) the formal parameter names are `LEFT` and `RIGHT` (binary operator) or just `RIGHT` (unary operator).

The exceptions that can be raised by the operators are summarised in Table 23.

7.3 Simple expressions

A **simple expression** is one that does not involve any of

and **or** **xor** **not** **and then** **or else**
= /= < <= > >= **in** **not in**

at the outer parenthesis level. Any expression can be converted to a simple expression by enclosing it in parentheses. Simple expressions are required in a number of places, e.g. for the bounds of a range (section 4.1.4).

Table 21 Operands

form of operand	example	section
names:		
identifier	I, param_2	2.2
expanded name	K.I, K.'A'	7
indexed component	A(1,I+2)	6.1.3
slice	A(1..J+1)	6.1.3
selected component	R.C	6.2.8
allocated object	P.**all**	6.3.5
literals:		
numeric literal	32, 5.3625	5.1
character literal	'C'	4.3
enumeration identifier	PERSIAN	4.2
string literal	"String"	4.3.1
aggregates:		
record aggregate	(C=>1,D=>2)	6.2.7
array aggregate	(1..10=>5)	6.1.4
others:		
type conversion	T(E)	3.3.4
qualified expression	T'(E)	3.3.5
allocator	**new** S	6.3.6
function call	F(A,B+2)	12.2.2

Table 22 Operators etc.

operator	type of L	type of R	result type
logical operators, precedence = 1 (section 4.4.1):			
L **and** R, L **or** R, L **xor** R	boolean scalar or 1-dimensional boolean array	same as L	same as L
short-circuit control forms, precedence = 1 (section 4.4.1):			
L **and then** R, L **or else** R	boolean	same as L	same as L
relational operators , precedence = 2 (section 4.1.2):			
L = R, L /= R	any	same as L	BOOLEAN
L < R, L <= R, L > R, L >= R	scalar or discrete array	same as L	BOOLEAN
membership tests, precedence = 2 (section 4.1.4):			
L **in** R, L **not in** R	any	range or subtype	BOOLEAN
binary adding operators, precedence = 3 (sections 5.2.3, 5.4.4, 5.5.3, 6.1.5):			
L + R, L - R	any numeric	same as L	same as L
L & R	discrete array or component	discrete array or component	discrete array
unary adding operators, precedence = 4 (sections 5.2.3, 5.4.4, 5.5.3):			
+ R, - R		any numeric	same as R

Table 22 (continued) Operators etc.

operator	type of L	type of R	result type
multiplying operators, precedence = 5 (sections 5.2.3, 5.4.4, 5.5.3):			
L * R, L / R	integer	same as L	same as L
L * R, L / R	floating point	same as L	same as L
L * R, L / R	fixed point	INTEGER	same as L
L * R	INTEGER	fixed point	same as R
L * R, L / R	fixed point	fixed point	*universal_fixed*
L * R, L / R	*universal_real*	*universal_integer*	*universal_real*
L * R	*universal_integer*	*universal_real*	*universal_real*
L **mod** R, L **rem** R	integer	same as L	same as L
highest precedence operators, precedence = 6 (sections 5.2.3, 5.4.4, 5.5.3, 4.4.1):			
L ** R	integer	integer	same as L
L ** R	floating point	integer	same as L
L **abs** R	numeric	same as L	same as L
not R		boolean scalar or 1-dimensional boolean array	same as L

Table 23 Exceptions raised by operators

operator	exception	when raised
and, **or**, **xor**	CONSTRAINT_ ERROR	boolean array operands of different lengths
+, -, *, /, **mod**, **rem**, **	NUMERIC_ ERROR	result outside range of integer type, or outside range of safe numbers of real type
/, **mod**, **rem**	NUMERIC_ ERROR	right operand is zero
**	CONSTRAINT_ ERROR	left operand integer and right operand zero
&	CONSTRAINT_ ERROR	component operand not in component subtype, or upper bound of non-null result outside index subtype

7.4 Static expressions

Static expressions are those which every Ada compiler must evaluate at compile time; a static expression is required in various situations, e.g. as a case expresssion (section 8.4).

An expression is static if all the following are true:

(1) it is of a scalar type,
(2) it includes only predefined operators,
(3) its evaluation does not raise an exception,
(4) every operand is one of:
- a literal or named number,
- a constant with static subtype and static initial expression,
- a function call to a predefined operator with static actual parameters,
- a language-defined attribute of a static subtype (with static actual parameter if a function),
- a qualified expression with static subtype and expression.

A compiler may evaluate other expressions at compile-time, but the results must be the same as if evaluated at run-time. Other constructs which may be required to be static are as follows.

(1) A *range* (section 4.1.4) is static if it is of the explicit form `L..U` and its bounds `L` and `U` are static expressions

(2) A *subtype* (section 3.3.2) is static if it is one of:

- a discrete subtype, unconstrained or with a static range constraint
- a real type, unconstrained or with one of:
- a static range constraint
- a floating point or fixed point constraint with no range constraint or with a static range constraint.

(3) A *discrete range* (section 4.1.4) is static if it is a static range or a static subtype indication.

(4) A *constraint* (section 3.3.2) is static if it is one of:

- a range constraint with a static range
- an index constraint of an array type with static index subtypes, and with all its discrete ranges static
- a *discriminant constraint* (section 6.2.3) of a record type with static discriminant subtypes, each expression being static.

7.5 Universal expressions

A **universal expression** has a result of type *universal_integer* (section 5.2) or *universal_real* (section 5.4). The operators are as for any other predefined integer or real types, and mixed *universal_integer* and *universal_real* multiplication and division are also available (see Table 22). An operand of universal type must be

- a numeric literal (section 5.1)
- a named number (section 3.4.2)
- an attribute delivering a universal result (section 1.4)

Universal expressions may be non-static (e.g. those involving attributes of arrays). Evaluation of static *universal_real* expressions is exact; that of non-static *universal_real* expressions is at least as accurate as for any other predefined floating point type. There is no limit to the values of static universal expressions, while for non-static universal expressions the values may be limited by the implementation but must cover at least SYSTEM.MIN_INT .. SYSTEM.MAX_INT (*universal_integer*) or the range of safe numbers of all other predefined real types (*universal_real*): NUMERIC_ERROR is raised if the range is violated.

8 Statements

Statements are summarised in Table 24 with references to where they are described. **Compound statements** contain embedded sequences of one or more statements, which may be of any kind, simple or compound.

This chapter describes the unspecialised sequential and control statements.

Every statement must be terminated by a semicolon. There is no empty statement in Ada; when a statement is required that does nothing (for instance in a case statement) use the **null statement**

```
null;
```

Table 24 Statements

simple	section	compound	section
sequential:			
null	8	block	8.5
assignment	8.1		
code	12.5		
control:			
exit	8.4	if	8.2
goto	8.6	case	8.3
raise	9.2	loop	8.4
return	12.1.2,12.2.2		
procedure call	12.1.3		
tasking:			
entry call	13.3.1	accept	13.3.1
delay	13.3.4	selective wait	13.3.2
abort	13.3.5	timed and conditional entry calls	13.3.3

8.1 Assignment statements

An **assignment statement** sets the value of a variable. It has the form

```
V := E;
```

The variable name `V` and the expression `E` must both have the same type, which can be any scalar, array, record, or access type, or a nonlimited private type. The variable can be a declared variable, a component or slice of an array, a component of a record, or the object designated by an access value (using **`.all`**). For the various forms of variable names see section 7.1.

On execution, the variable name and the expression are evaluated in undefined order, and the expression value is checked as follows. For arrays (including `STRING`) the expression value is checked to have the same number of dimensions and of elements in each dimension as the variable, though the bounds need not be the same. For other types, the expression value is checked to belong to the subtype of the variable. If the check succeeds the expression value is assigned to the variable (component by component for records and arrays), otherwise `CONSTRAINT_ERROR` is raised.

Note that as both sides are evaluated before the assignment there is no problem with overlapping slices: after

```
A : STRING(1 .. 8) := "MUREDXYZ";
A(4 .. 8) := A(1 .. 5);
```

`A` has the value `"MURMURED"`.

Note also that assignment to just a discriminant of a record is illegal; assignment to a whole record including discriminants is allowed only if the record type was declared with default values for the discriminants, and the record variable was declared or created without explicit discriminant values. See section 6.2.3.

8.2 If statements

An **if statement** allows a general choice of action (or no action). It has the form

```
if C then
   S;
   ... ;
{elsif C then
   S;
   ... ;}
[else
   S;
   ... ;]
end if;
```

Each **condition** C is a boolean expression (i.e. of type BOOLEAN or a type derived from it).

On execution, the conditions C are evaluated in order until one yields TRUE or **else** is reached, when the following statements S are executed; or until **end if** is reached, in which case nothing happens.

8.3 Case statements

A **case statement** allows a choice of action according to the value of a discrete expression. It has the form

```
case E is
  when X | ... =>
    S;
    ...;
  ...;
end case;
```

Each choice X is a static simple expression (standing for its value) or a static discrete range (standing for all the values in the range, including end-points), except that the choice **others** (standing for all values not otherwise mentioned) is allowed on its own as the final alternative.

The expression E and the choices X must be of a discrete type (enumeration or integer) determinable from E; any ambiguity can be removed by qualifying the E with the desired type (section 3.3.5).

The values of all the choices X must be different. If there is no **others** choice then every possible value of E (and no other values) must occur in a choice: i.e. in general every value of the type of E, but if E is an object of a static subtype (section 7.3), or a type conversion or qualified expression with a static subtype, then only the values of the subtype.

As the choices are static, these checks are all made at compile time.

On execution, the expression E is evaluated and the sequence of statements S following the choice for that value is executed.

8.4 Loop statements

A **loop statement** allows repeated action. It has one of the forms

```
[L :]
  loop
    S;
    ...;
  end loop [L];

[L :]
  while C loop
    S;
    ...;
  end loop [L];

[L :]
  for I in [reverse] R loop
    S;
    ...;
  end loop [L];
```

The loop name L is an identifier used as a prefix within the loop for the loop parameter I (section 7.1), and as operand of an exit statement.

In the first case the sequence of statements S is executed repeatedly until an exit statement us met (or some other event intervenes).

In the second case the condition C is evaluated before each execution of the S (including the first such execution), and execution of the loop stops as soon as it is found to be FALSE.

In the third case, the discrete range R is evaluated and then the statements S are executed once with each value in the discrete range assigned to the identifier (if **reverse** is present the range is traversed in reverse order; if the range is empty, the statements are not executed at all). The identifier I, called the loop parameter, acts in the loop like a local constant: it cannot be assigned to, or used as a parameter of mode **out** or **in out** (section 12.1.1), and does not exist outside the loop.

The loop parameter `I` takes its type and subtype from the discrete range `R`. In particular, if `R` is static, so is `I`'s subtype - this can affect e.g. its use in a case statement expression. If the type of `R` is ambiguous (e.g. because of overloaded enumeration literals) the ambiguity can be removed by qualifying one of the bounds, or by mentioning the type explicitly in the range (section 4.1.4).

To leave a loop (of any form) at any point, use an **exit statement**:

```
exit [L] [when C];
```

This is only allowed inside a loop statement (only inside the named loop if a loop name `L` is given). The condition `C`, if there is one, is evaluated; if its value is `TRUE` (or if there is no condition) control is transferred to just after the **end if** of the named loop statement, or of the smallest enclosing loop statement if there is no loop name.

8.5 Block statements

A **block statement** groups together a sequence of statements, possibly with local declarations and exception handlers (section 9.1) into a single statement. It is one form of *frame* (section 1.10). Its form is

```
[B :]
   [declare
      declarative_part]
   begin
      statement;
      ...;
   [exception
      exception_handler;
      ...;]
   end [B];
```

The block name `B` is an identifier used within the block statement as a prefix (section 7.1) for identifiers declared in the declarative part.

The declarations in the declarative part, if any, are elaborated in order (section 3.1), then the statements are executed. The exception handlers, if any, apply to exceptions arising during execution of the statements.

Entities declared within a block statement are **local** to it, i.e. they can be referred to directly only within the block statement, and cease to exist once control leaves it.

8.6 Goto statements and labels

Control is explicitly transferred to another point in the program by a **goto statement**

```
goto L;
```

where the label L is an identifier prefixed to the target statement:

```
<<L>>
    statement;
```

The scope (section 3.2.1) of the label L is the statements and exception handlers of the innermost enclosing frame.

A goto statement can transfer control within or out of, but not into, any of the following: the sequence of statements in a loop statement; the alternative arms of a case statement, an if statement, or a select statement or the sequence of statements and individual exception handlers of a block statement or other frame. Note that labels are not the same as loop and block names - only labels can be used in goto statements. Nonetheless all labels, loop names, and block names in any program unit body (section 1.10) must be distinct.

9 Exceptions

Exceptions enable the program to detect and deal with an error or other exceptional event. Such errors as numeric overflow can be detected and dealt with; the programmer can also define his own exceptions and handle them in the same way. However, it is impossible to return to the place where the exception occurred; execution must continue in some outer construct.

9.1 Exception handlers

An **exception handler** resembles a case statement in form, and prescribes the action to be taken on the occurrence of specified exceptions within its scope. This scope is the sequence of statements in the innermost enclosing *frame* (section 1.10), i.e. block statement, subprogram body, package body, or task body. A generic body is counted as a subprogram or package body at each instantiation. If a frame has exception handlers, they are all gathered together at the end:

```
heading
   declarative_item;
   ...;
begin
   statement;
   ...;
exception
   exception_handler;
   ...;
end;
```

If there are no exception handlers, then the reserved word **exception** is omitted.

An exception handler has a form like an element of a case statement:

```
when
   X|... =>
      statement;
      ...;
```

Each exception choice X is the name of an exception, except that the choice **others** (standing for all exceptions not explicitly mentioned, whether visible or not) is allowed on its own as the only choice of the last exception handler of a frame. All the exception names in all the handlers in a frame must denote different exceptions. The effect of raising an exception is as follows.

(1) During the statements of a frame with a handler for that exception: the statements of that handler are executed, after which the frame is abandoned; the program continues as if the frame had terminated normally.

(2) During the statements of a frame with no handler for the exception, or in the declarative part or exception handlers when the frame is not a task body:

- if the frame is not the main program or a library task body, the exception is **propagated**, i.e. the frame is abandoned and the exception is reraised at:
  - the point of call of a subprogram (other than the main program)
  - immediately after a block statement
  - immediately after a package body (other than a library package), or after the body stub if it is a subunit (section 10.2).
- if the frame is the main program or a library package, the program is abandoned (and the implementation should provide some form of diagnostic message).

An exception is not propagated out of a subprogram (including the main program) or a block statement until all dependent tasks are terminated (section 13.2). It is undefined whether the same is true of a library package (a non-library package has no dependent tasks to wait for).

(3) During the statements of a task body with no handler for it, or in the exception handlers: the task is normally just completed, there is no propagation. However, an exception in the called task during a rendezvous is (if not handled) propagated both to the calling task at the point of call and to the called task just after the accept statement, the accept statement being abandoned.

(4) During the declarative part of a task body: the task becomes completed and TASKING_ERROR is raised at the point of activation.

(5) During a task or non-library package declaration: the exception is propagated to the enclosing declarative part or package specification, immediately after the task or package declaration.

(6) During a library package declaration: the program is abandoned (preferably with a diagnostic message).

9.2 Raise statements

Any exception X may be explicitly raised by a **raise statement**

```
raise X;
```

A special form of raise statement, allowed only within an exception handler, is

```
raise;
```

This causes the exception which invoked the handler to be raised again. This is particularly useful with **others** when it is desired to propagate the exception after, for instance, generating an error message; there is no other way to tell which exception was raised.

9.3 Exception declarations

There are five *predefined exceptions* (see below) which are raised on specific occasions during execution of the program. Other exceptions can be declared in the program and raised explicitly: this gives a powerful well-structured way of dealing with exceptional occurrences in the execution of the program.

An **exception declaration** has the form

```
X, ... : exception;
```

where a multiple declaration is equivalent to several exception declarations (section 1.8), i.e. it declares several different exceptions. Repeated elaboration of an exception declaration (e.g. in a recursive subprogram) does not yield distinct exceptions, but an exception declaration in a generic unit defines different exceptions in each instantiation.

As well as the predefined exceptions, effectively declared in package STANDARD (section 16.1.10), there are exceptions defined in other standard library packages: TIME_ERROR in package CALENDAR (section 16.2.1) and the input-output exceptions in package IO_EXCEPTIONS (section 15.3).

9.4 Predefined exceptions

The **predefined exceptions** are shown in Table 25. Each of them is raised on the failure of one of a number of particular checks carried out during program execution. Some of these checks may not be implemented (if there is no hardware support and implementation by software would be prohibitively costly) though any such omission should be noted in the User's Guide.

Permission to suppress some checks, to improve run-time performance, can be selectively given to the compiler (but may be ignored) by use of the language-defined pragma

```
pragma SUPPRESS(check);
```

or

```
pragma SUPPRESS(check, [ON =>] name);
```

The check is one of the check names from Table 25, the name is an identifier or expanded name, and the presence of 'ON =>' makes no difference. The pragma may appear:

(1) in a declarative part, when its effect extends from the pragma to the end of the enclosing frame
(2) in a package specification, when it must include the name of an entity declared previously in the package specification; its effect extend from the pragma to the end of the declarations's scope (section 3.2.1).

If there is a name, the effect is restricted to:

- operations on the named object
- operations on objects of the base type of the named type or subtype
- calls of the named subprogram
- activations of tasks of the named task type
- instantiations of the named generic unit.

No other names are allowed.

If the check is suppressed but would have failed, the program is erroneous.

Table 25 Predefined exceptions

check:	check fails when:
for exception CONSTRAINT_ERROR *(name is object or type):*	
ACCESS_CHECK	access to an allocated object is via null access value.
DISCRIMINANT_CHECK	discriminant value does not satisfy constraint; accessed record component in a variant does not exist.
INDEX_CHECK	bounds of array are unequal to those of index constraint: index value does not satisfy constraint; index bounds of slice do not satisfy constraint.
LENGTH_CHECK	array lengths are unequal in assignment, type conversion, or predefined boolean operator.
RANGE_CHECK	scalar value does not satisfy range constraint; subtype constraint is incompatible with type mark in subtype indication; index or discriminant in aggregate is not within subtype; generic actual parameter does not match generic formal parameter in generic instantiation.
for exception NUMERIC_ERROR *(name is numeric type):*	
DIVISION_CHECK	second operand of /, **rem**, or **mod** is zero
OVERFLOW_CHECK	result of numeric operation is outside capacity of type (may not be fully implemented - see section 5.3).

Table 25 (continued) Predefined exceptions

check	when check fails
for exception PROGRAM_ERROR *(name is task unit, generic unit, or subprogram):*	
ELABORATION_ CHECK	body has not been elaborated when subprogram called, generic unit instantiated, or task activated.
(not suppresible)	end of function reached; no open alternative or **else** part in selective wait; erroneous action detected.
for exception STORAGE_ERROR *(name is access type, task unit, or subprogram):*	
STORAGE_CHECK	no space available for allocated object, declared object, subprogram call, or task activation.
for exception TASKING_ERROR*:*	
(not suppressible)	called task is completed before entry call is accepted; called task aborted during rendezvous; exception in declarative part of task being activated.

10 Compilation and Program Structure

10.1 Compilation units and the program library

10.1.1 Compilation

The unit of compilation is the *compilation unit*. A sequence of compilation units submitted to the compiler at one time is called a **compilation**. The compilation units can be interspersed with pragmas, affecting the preceding unit or the compilation as a whole. Indeed a compilation can consist just of pragmas, with no compilation units. The language-defined pragmas that can appear at this level are as follows.

(1) Before the first compilation unit, or alone in the compilation:

```
pragma MEMORY_SIZE(N);
pragma STORAGE_UNIT(N);
pragma SYSTEM_NAME(L);
```

These reset system-dependent values - see section 16.2.2

(2) After a library subprogram declaration P (sections 12.4, 12.5):

```
pragma INLINE(P);
pragma INTERFACE(P,L);
```

(3) Before, after, or between compilation units:

```
pragma LIST(ON);      -- turn compilation listing on
pragma LIST(OFF);     -- turn compilation listing off
pragma PAGE;          -- start a new page on the
                      -- compilation listing
```

The pragmas in group (3) are also allowed anywhere else that a pragma is allowed (section 1.5); the pragmas themselves are always listed.

Another pragma provided to affect the compilation process, which may appear only in a declarative part, is OPTIMIZE. This requests the compiler to compile the surrounding body or block so as to minimise execution time or space:

```
pragma OPTIMIZE(TIME);  -- minimise execution time
pragma OPTIMISE(SPACE); -- minimise execution space
```

10.1.2 Compilation units

For most purposes the compilation units in a compilation can be regarded as being presented to the compiler one at a time. An important concept is the **program library**; this is a collection of compilation units that have been successfully compiled, and it is in the context of the program library that a compilation unit is compiled.

A **compilation unit** is either a *library unit* or a *secondary unit.*

A **library unit** is any of:

- a subprogram declaration
- a subprogram body without a separate declaration
- a package declaration
- a generic declaration
- a generic instantiation

Compiling a unit introduces it to the program library, or reintroduces it if it has been previously compiled. All library units in a program library must have different identifiers

A **secondary unit** is one of:

- the body of a package ot subprogram, the declaration of which has already been compiled;
- a subunit (see below).

Compilation of a secondary unit does not introduce or reintroduce a unit to the program lirary.

10.2 Subunits

A **subunit** is the separately compiled body of a subprogram (not an operator), package, or task.

The corresponding specification must occur as a declarative item in a compilation unit (possibly another subunit), called the **parent unit;** the body is replaced within the parent unit by a **body stub**

```
procedure P [formal part] is separate;

function F [formal part] result T is separate;

package body P is separate;

task body T is separate;
```

The subunit itself has the form

```
separate (P)
B;
```

where B is a subprogram, package, or task body, and P is the name of the parent unit. If the parent unit is a library unit, P is just its identifier; otherwise it has the form

```
P1.P2. ... .Pn
```

where each Pi is an identifier: Pi is the parent of P(i+1), Pn is the parent of the subunit in question, and P1 is a library unit (the **ancestor unit**). All subunits of the same ancestor unit must have different identifiers, but subunits of different ancestors need not. The visibility of declarations in a subunit is exactly as though the subunit replaced the body stub in the parent unit, and any context clause preceding the subunit were merged with the context clause of the parent unit.

10.3 Context clauses and dependences

Any compilation unit may be preceded by a **context clause**

```
with U,...;
```

or

```
with U,...; use V,...;
```

Here the U are the identifiers of library units which are to be made visible to the following compilation unit, and in the second case the V are the identifiers of library packages from among the U.

The use clause has the effect of making the declarations in the visible parts of the specifications of the V *directly visible* (if not hidden) – see section 3.2.2. If the compilation unit is a library unit, the scope of the context clause includes the corresponding body, if there is one, and any of its subunits. If the compilation unit is a secondary unit, the context clause applies only within it.

A compilation unit **depends** on the specifications of the library units mentioned in its context clause; that is to say, if any of them is altered in the program library (e.g. by recompilation) then the dependent unit becomes invalid, and cannot be used to form a program (unless the compiler can detect that the alterations cannot affect then meaning of the dependent unit). Also, a compilation unit cannot be compiled until all the units it depends on have been compiled (and not subsequently invalidated). This means that the compilation order of a large program may need to be carefully thought out.

Dependences can arise in other ways, see Table 26.

Table 26 Dependences

dependence	dependent unit	unit depended on
with	compilation unit A preceded by with clause naming B	library unit B named in A's with clause
body/spec	body of library unit A	specification of A
inline	(1) unit containing call to inlined subprogram B (2) unit containing call to inlined subprogram in package P	body of subprogram B body of package P
parent	subunit A of library unit B	parent B of subunit A
generic	instantiation A of generic unit B	body of generic unit B

10.4 Programs

A **program** consists of one or more library units (including any subsidiary predefined library units required – see section 16.2), with their secondary units. One of these library units is a library subprogram containing the entry point to the program; this is the **main program**. The other library units of the program are those *withed* by those library units; and so on.

The compiler may (and usually does) put restrictions on the parameters and results of a subprogram to be used as a main program; the minimum is to allow just parameterless procedures.

10.4.1 Elaboration order

Every declaration in a program must be elaborated before the declared entity can be used, and the declarations and bodies of library units are no exception. (A subunit is elaborated at the elaboration of its body stub.) The order in which these compilation units are elaborated must satisfy the following rules.

(1) The specification of a library unit is elaborated before its body.

(2) The specification of any library unit mentioned in the context clause of a compilation unit is elaborated before that compilation unit.

(3) The specification of any library unit mentioned in the context clause of a subunit is elaborated before the body of the subunit's ancestor unit.

Additional ordering constraints may be imposed by using pragma `ELABORATE`:

```
pragma ELABORATE(U,...);
```

This goes after the context clause and before the compilation unit. The identifiers `U` are those of library units mentioned in the context clause. The effect is to constrain the elaboration order so that the *bodies* of the library units `U` are elaborated before the following compilation unit. This may be needed e.g. to ensure that a library subprogram may be called from the body of a library package.

If no elaboration order for the compilation units can be found, the program is illegal.

10.4.2 Structure of a program

The library units of a program act as if declared within the predefined package STANDARD (section 16.1). The following model of a program shows this explicitly. The whole program is embedded in an environment task.

```
task body ENVIRONMENT_TASK is
begin
  MAIN_BLOCK:
    declare
      package STANDARD is
        -- See section 16.1
      end STANDARD;
      package body STANDARD is
        -- If main program is a function: declaration of a
        -- variable R of the result type.
        -- If main program has any parameters,
        -- declarations of variables V, ... of the formal
        -- parameter types.
        -- Declarations of library units and secondary units
        -- with the needed by the program, in an order
        -- consistent elaboration order defined above.
        -- Declaration of main program (library
        -- subprogram specification and body).
      begin
        -- Implementation-defined statements to obtain the
        -- actual parameters A, ... (if any) to the main
        -- program.
        -- Assignment statements for all in and
        -- in out parameters: V := A;
        -- If the main program is a procedure P, a
        -- procedure call statement: P(V, ...);
        -- else if the main program is a function F, an
        -- assignment statement: R := F(V, ...);
      end STANDARD;
    begin
      null;
    exception
      -- Implementation-defined handlers for all exceptions
      -- that may be raised by elaboration of library units
      -- or execution of the main program.
```

```
        end MAIN_BLOCK;
      -- Implementation-defined statements to close any open
      -- external files and return result of main program, if a
      -- function.
      -- Assignment statements for all in out and out
      -- parameters: A := V;
      -- ENVIRONMENT_TASK now waits for any unterminated
      -- tasks (the library tasks, section 13.1) to terminate,
      -- before itself terminating.
    end ENVIRONMENT_TASK;
```

11 Packages

Packages allow groups of related entities to be declared together, so that they can be used from other parts of the program while their internal structure is hidden. A package is defined in two parts, a *specification* and a *body,* though the body may be absent.

11.1 Package specifications

A *package specification* is declared by a **package declaration** with the form

```
package P is
   B1;
   ...;
[private
   B2;
   ...;]
end [P];
```

where each B is a *basic declaration* (section 3.1.1), a *representation clause* (section 1.6), or a *use clause* (section 3.2.4). (The **package specification** is just the package declaration without the terminating semicolon.) The entities declared in `B1; ...;` (the **visible part** of the package) are visible from outside the package as well as within the package specification and body. The entities declared in `B2; ...;` (the **private part** of the package) are visible only within the private part and the package body, not from outside the package – they are needed to allow the compiler to compile certain references correctly.

11.2 Package bodies

A **package body** is required if the package specification contains an incomplete declaration of an entity (see Table 27); otherwise a package body is not needed (though one can always be given). A package body declaration (called simply a *package body*) has the form

```
package body P is
   [declarative_part]
[begin
   statement;
   ...;
[exception
   exception_handler;]]
   ...;
end [P];
```

Table 27 Package specification and body

package specification contains:	package body contains:	section
subprogram specification	subprogram body	12
package specification	package body (if given)	11
task declaration	task body	13.1
generic declaration	generic body (if given)	14.1
incomplete type declaration in private part	full type or task type declaration (if not in package specification)	6.3.2

Note: A subprogram, package or task body may be replaced by a body stub in the package body and a separately compiled subunit (section 10.2).

11.3 Private types

A type can be declared in the visible part of a package specification as a **private type**:

```
type T [(D;...)] is private;
```

Here the D are *discriminant specifications* (section 6.2.3). There must be a corresponding full type declaration in the private part:

```
type T [(D;...)] is type_definition;
```

If the private type declaration has discriminants D then so must the full type declaration (which must therefore be a record type declaration), and the two discriminant parts must *conform* (section 1.9).

Outside the package, the type mark T can be used only for the following:

(1) to declare an object of type T
(2) to declare an access type to objects of type T:

```
type U is access T;
```

(3) in the attributes T'BASE, T'SIZE, and T'CONSTRAINED

and the only operations available on an object X of type T (whether declared or created by allocators) are

- assignment X := E;
- membership tests X **in** S, X **not in** S
- selection of a discriminant X.D
- predefined comparisons X=Y, X/=Y
- subprograms declared in the visible part of the package with parameters and/or results of type T

A **limited private type** is declared as follows:

```
type T [(D;...)] is limited private;
```

In this case the type can be fully defined in the private part either by a full type declaration

```
type T [(D;...)] is type_definition;
```

or by a task type declaration

```
task type T [is
   entry_declaration;
   ...;
   [address_clause;
   ...;]
end [T]];
```

The operations available outside the package are the same except that assignment and predefined comparisons are not allowed (but the comparison operators can be *overloaded*, see section 12.3).

11.4 Deferred constant declarations

A **deferred constant declaration** allows a constant of a private type to be declared. It has the form

```
I, ... : constant T;
```

where `T` is the type mark of a private type, or of a subtype of a private type. For multiple declarations see section 1.8. The deferred constant declaration must appear in the visible part of the same package specification as, and after, the private type declaration for `T` or the base type of `T`.

There must be a corresponding full constant declaration in the private part, after the full type declaration for the private type:

```
I, ... : constant T := E;
```

If multiple declarations are used, they do not have to correspond exactly, but the equivalent single declarations must do so.

Between the deferred constant declaration and the corresponding full declaration, the identifier `I` may be used only in a default expression, for a record component or (non-generic) formal parameter. After the full declaration, and outside the package specification, it may be used in the same ways as any constant.

12 Subprograms

A **subprogam** is a fragment of a program which can be called repeatedly from elsewhere in the program. Subprograms are *functions* (which return results) and *procedures* (which do not). Procedures are described first.

12.1 Procedures

12.1.1 Procedure declarations

A **procedure** P is declared by a **procedure declaration**:

```
procedure P [(I, ... : [mode] T [:= E]; ...)];
```

The **formal part**

```
(I, ... : [mode] T [:= E]; ...)
```

specifies the **formal parameters** I of the procedure; these are replaced by actual parameters on the call of the procedure. Multiple parameter specifications are treated as described in section 1.8.

Each formal parameter has a mode, and a type and subtype defined by the type mark T. A formal parameter of mode **in** (see below) may also have a default initial value given by an expression E, of the base type of T; these expressions must not contain any of the formal parameters, and are not evaluated until the subprogram is called.

There are 3 **modes** of formal parameters: **in**, **out**, and **in out**; roughly, **in** indicates that the actual parameter can be evaluated or read, **out** that its value can be updated. See Table 28 for more details. The default mode is **in**.

Table 28 Formal parameters

mode	(sub)type (see note 1)	binding method	constraint check (see note 1)	notes
in	scalar	copy-in	inward	
in	composite	copy-in or ref	inward	(2)
in	task	copy-in or ref	inward	(3)
in	access	copy-in	inward	(4)
in out	scalar	copy-in & back	inward & outward	
in out	composite	copy-in & back or ref	inward	(2)
in out	task	copy-in or ref	inward	(3)
in out	access	copy-in & back	inward & outward	
out	scalar	copy-back	outward	
out	composite	copy-back or ref	inward	(2,5)
out	task	NOT ALLOWED (task types are limited - sec. 13.1)		
out	access	copy-in & back	outward	

Notes

(1) Binding methods and constraint checks refer to actual parameter passing during subprogram calls.

(2) No outward check is needed for a constrained parameter subtype, as the bounds or discriminants cannot change. Neither check is needed for an unconstrained parameter subtype, as a formal array parameter is constrained with the actual parameter's bounds and a formal record parameter has the same constraints or lack of them as the actual parameter.

(3) The value of the formal parameter denotes the same task as the actual parameter, whichever binding method is used.

(4) Even though the actual parameter can only be read, the allocated value can be read and updated.

(5) If copy-back is used, the bounds, discriminants, and access type components of the actual parameter and its subcomponents are copied in at the start of the call.

12.1.2 *Procedure bodies*

The piece of program text to be executed is given in a **procedure body**:

```
procedure P [(I,...  : [mode] T [:= E];...)] is
   [declarative_part]
begin
   S;
   ...;
[exception
   exception_handler;
   ...;]
end [P];
```

For the *declarative part*, see section 3.1.1; for the *exception handlers* see section 9.1.

The separate procedure declaration is optional; it is needed only if the procedure is declared in a package (so that the body is in the package body) or if it is one of a set of mutually recursive subprograms. If both a declaration and a body are given then the specifications (up to the end of the formal part) must *conform* (section 1.9). Also the body must be after the declaration, and in the same declarative part or, if the declaration is in a package specification (section 11.1), in the declarative part of the package body.

Execution of the procedure body terminates

(1) by raising an exception which is not handled within the body (section 9.1)

(2) by reaching the end of the statements or of an exception handler

(3) by executing a **return statement** (not allowed within an enclosed task or package body):

```
return;
```

The last two are called *normal termination.*

12.1.3 *Procedure calls*

A procedure is invoked by a **procedure call statement**:

```
P [([I =>] A, ...) ];
```

where each *parameter association* is an actual parameter A (positional association) or

```
I => A
```

where I is a formal parameter identifier (named association). The association rules are as in section 1.7 except that multiple associations and **others** are not allowed, and parameters with default expressions need not appear (all parameter associations following a defaulted parameter must be named).

An actual parameter A is as follows (T is the formal parameter's type):

(1) formal parameter mode **in**: an expression of type T

(2) formal parameter mode **in out** or **out**: a variable name V (declared variable, slice, allocated object, or indexed or selected component (not a discriminant)), of type T, or a *type conversion* (section 3.3.4) of such a variable name to type T:

```
T(V)
```

The effect of executing the procedure call statement is as follows.

(1) The following actions are performed in an undefined order:
- the actual parameter expressions or variable names are evaluated (including any default expressions for missing parameters)
- any **in out** parameters which are type conversions are converted to the formal parameter type
- any inward constraint checks are performed (see below)
- any copy-in bindings of the actual parameters are performed (see below).

(2) The procedure body is executed.

(3) If the procedure terminates normally (see above), the following actions are performed in an undefined order:
- for any **in out** or **out** parameters which are type conversions, the formal parameter value is converted to the actual parameter's type
- any outward constraint checks are performed
- any copy-back bindings are performed
- execution continues after the procedure call.

If the procedure terminates by an unhandled exception, these actions

are not performed; control is returned to the local *exception handlers* (section 9.1).
The binding method (Table 28) is the method of passing the actual parameter's value to the procedure:

(1) copy-in = the value of the actual parameter is copied to the formal parameter at the start of the call
(2) copy-back = the value of the formal parameter is copied to the actual parameter at the end of the call
(3) ref(erence) = every use of the formal parameter is interpreted as denoting the actual parameter.

In the absence of aliasing (reference to an actual parameter via another actual parameter or a global variable) the binding method makes no difference. Aliasing is legal but reliance on binding method is erroneous.
The constraint checks (Table 28) are as follows.

(1) Inward: the actual parameter value is checked to belong to the formal parameter's subtype
(2) Outward: the formal parameter's value is checked to belong to the actual parameter's subtype.

If the value is undefined, the program is erroneous. If the check fails, `CONSTRAINT_ERROR` is raised at the procedure call.

12.2 Functions

12.2.1 Function declarations

A **function** `F` is declared by a **function declaration**

```
function F(I,...:[mode] T [:=E],...) return R;
```

Here `R` is a type mark for the type or subtype of the returned value. `F` can be either an identifier or an **operator symbol**, i.e. a string literal (section 4.3.1) for one of the predefined operators (for `"="` and `"/="` see below). The string literal must contain no spaces, but upper or lower case letters are equivalent: `"Mod"`, `"MOD"`, `"mod"` are all the same.
If `F` is an operator symbol, the function is an **operator**: there must

be the correct number (one or two, left operand first) of parameters, and no default expressions. The defined operator *overloads* the predefined operator (section 12.3). The short circuit control forms **and then** and **or else**, and the membership tests **in** and **not in** are not operators and cannot be redeclared in this way. There are also restrictions on the redeclaration of equality and inequality:

(1) equality "=" can only be declared as

```
function "=" (L,R : T) return BOOLEAN;
```

where L and R are any identifiers and T is a limited type.

(2) inequality "/=" cannot be declared at all, but is implicitly declared by the above declaration of "=" as follows (shown as a comment as it is not legal Ada):

```
-- function "/=" (L,R:T) return BOOLEAN is
--    begin
--      return not (L = R);
-- end "/=";
```

The formal part of a function declaration is as for a procedure except that the only parameter mode allowed is **in**.

As with a procedure, a function body can be declared separately:

```
function F(I,... : [in] T [:= E], ...)
return R is
   [declarative part]
begin
    statement;
    ...;
[exception
    exception handler;]
    ...;
end [F];
```

As with a procedure, a separate function declaration is not required unless needed; if one is given the function specification must *conform* (section 1.9).

The result of a functon is returned to the call by a **return statement** not within the body of an enclosed task or package):

```
return E;
```

where E is an expression of the result type R'BASE. The expression E is evaluated and checked to belong to the result subtype R; CONSTRAINT_ERROR is raised if the check fails. The function then terminates and execution continues after the function call.

A function must terminate with a result statement, or by raising an exception. If it reaches the end of the body with neither of these having happened, PROGRAM_ERROR is raised at the call.

12.2.2 Function calls

A function call is an *operand* (section 7.1), and yields a result; it has one of the forms

```
F                        -- no parameters
F ([I =>] A, ...);       -- with parameters A, ...
```

For an operator the prefix or infix form typified by

```
-X      X+Y
```

is generally used. Precedences are the same as for the predefined operators (section 7.1). The functional form can also be used if desired, even for the predefined operators:

```
"-"(X)    "+"(LEFT => X, RIGHT => Y)
```

12.3 Overloading of subprogram names

The identifiers (and operator symbols) of subprograms can be **overloaded**, i.e. the same name can be used for more than one subprogram, all visible at the same place. If they have the same number and types of the formal parameters and (for a function) the same result type, they are *homographs* and one can hide the other (see section 3.2.3). In any case, homographs or not, for a call of a subprogram to be legal the following must identify the subprogram uniquely:

(1) whether it is a procedure or a function call
(2) the number and types of actual parameters provided

(3) (for a function) the result type expected
(4) any names of formal parameters used in named associations.

For the purpose of resolving overloading, enumeration literals are considered to be parameterless functions, and single entries of tasks are treated as procedures. For more details, see secton 3.2.3.

Ambiguous calls to overloaded subprograms can be disambiguated by:

- qualifying actual parameters or the function result
- using an expanded name, or renaming
- using named associations.

12.4 Inline expansion

Inline expansion of the code of a procedure can be requested by using the pragma INLINE

```
pragma INLINE(S,...);
```

where the S are the names of subprograms (or generic subprograms, see section 14.1) to be inlined. The pragma can be given after the declarations of the S, in the same declarative part or package specification, or immediately after a library subprogram (which must be the only subprogram mentioned).

The compiler may ignore the request (because inlining is not implemented, or is inefficient or impossible in this case).

12.5 Non-Ada subprograms

There are two ways provided for the use of subprograms written in other languages: pragma INTERFACE and package MACHINE_CODE. Neither, either, or both of these may be supported by an implementation.

The predefined pragma INTERFACE takes two arguments: the name of a language L and a subprogram name S:

```
pragma INTERFACE(L,S);
```

It must appear in the same package specification or declarative part as, and later than, the declaration of S; or, if S is a library subprogram, immediately after the declaration of S. Of course there must be no Ada body for S. The pragma tells the compilation system to compile calls to S appropriately for language L, and that a compiled body for S will be supplied externally. The available languages L and the means of supplying the body, as well as any restrictions on the use of alien subprograms (e.g. on parameter types) are implementation-defined.

Pragma INTERFACE may also be provided to allow the writing of subprogram bodies in matchine code (typically to assembler), so that the only effect is to warn the compiler to expect an external body; the machine code procedure must be accommodated to the Ada calling interface. Alternatively, an implementation may supply a predefined library package MACHINE_CODE: this defines one or more record types for the instruction formats of the machine, and usually ancillary entities, e.g. an enumeration type for function mnemonics. If package MACHINE_CODE is supplied, then a procedure (not a function) body can be written in machine code as follows:

(1) it must be within the scope of a context clause

```
with MACHINE_CODE;
```

(2) it must contain no declarations; only *use clauses* (section 3.2.4) may occur in the declarative part (if it has one)

(3) the only statements allowed are **code statements** with the form of qualified aggregates

```
T'(C,...);
```

where T is one of the types defined in package MACHINE_CODE, or a subtype of it, and the C are appropriate *component associations* (section 1.7)

(4) no exception handlers are allowed.

Allowable expressions in the component associations of code statements are implementation-defined. The implementation may provide further pragmas and/or attributes to assist in writing machine code procedures. For all these matters, consult your User's Guide.

13 Tasks

Tasks are parts of a program that can be executed (logically or actually) concurrently with each other. The main program forms one task; others are created explicitly by special language constructs. A task is defined by a **task unit**, comprising a *task specification* and a *task body*. A task is in effect a value of a *task type*. Task types are defined by task declarations, and objects of task types are created by object declarations and allocators in the usual way. A task which is the value of a task object is created at the same time as the task object, and the value of the task object cannot be changed thereafter.

13.1 Task types and subtypes

A **task type** T is defined by a **task declaration** of the form

```
task type T is
  [entry declaration;
  ...;]
  [representation clause;
  ...;]
end [T];
```

The **task specification** is the task declaration without the final semicolon.

The entry declarations and representation clauses are explained below. The execution of tasks of the task type T is defined by a **task body** of the form

```
task body T is
  [declarative_part]
begin
  statement;
  ...;
[exception
  exception_handler;
  ...;]
end [T];
```

Outside the task body, the identifier `T` denotes the task type declared by the task declaration. Inside the task body it denotes the task object with value the task currently executing the task body, and not the task type; it can also be used as a *prefix* (section 7.1) denoting the task unit.

Task types are limited types (section 3.3.1), so assignment (including use as an **out** parameter and initialisation) are not possible, and there are no predefined operators, not even = and /=.

Task subtypes can be defined, but there are no applicable constraints, so they are all unconstrained.

13.1.1 Task entries

An *entry declarations* in the task declaration has one of the forms

```
entry E;                  -- single entry, no parameters

entry E(F;...);           -- single entry, with parameters

entry E(R);               -- entry family, no parameters

entry E(R)(F;...);        -- entry family, with parameters
```

The first two forms define a **single entry** with identifier `E`. The last two forms define a **family** of entries indexed by the descrete range `R`, all with the same formal part. The formal parameter specifications `F` are as for *procedure declarations* (section 12.1). Entries correspond to accept statements in the task body (see below) and are the externally visible entry points to the task. Single entries are treated as procedures for *overload resolution* (section 3.2.3), and can be *renamed* as procedures (section 3.2.5). Entries of families cannot be overloaded or renamed. The discrete range `R` is evaluated first, and then the formal parameter specifications as for a procedure declaration.

The representation clauses are restricted to the form

```
for E use at A;
```

where the entry identifier `E` is that of a single entry (not one of a family) in the same task declaration, and `A` is a simple expression of type `SYSTEM.ADDRESS` (section 16.2.2). It associates the entry with an interrupt defined by the expression. At most one such representation clause may apply to each entry; such an entry is called an **interrupt entry** – see below.

13.1.2 Task objects

A **task object** is declared by a normal variable declaration

```
I, ... : T;
```

where T is a task type; or is created by an allocator, as in

```
type A is access T;
I : A := new T;
```

Initialisation of the declaration is not possible, as task types are limited types; but in both cases the task type T defines the initial value to be a new task of type T. A task object cannot be declared as a constant, though its value cannot in fact be changed.

Arrays and records with task subcomponents can be declared and created by allocators; a new task is created for each task type subcomponent.

The declaration of a task object and its type may be combined to form a task declaration (as for a task type but without **type**)

```
task T is
   [entry declaration;
   ...;]
   [representation clause;
   ...;]
end [T];
```

This declares an anonymous task type *A* and a single task T of that type:

```
task type A is
   [entry declaration;
   ...;]
   [representation clause;
   ...;]
end A;

T : A;
```

This requires a task body, as described above, with the identifier T. Inside the body, T denotes the current task object, or (as a prefix) the task unit, as above. Outside the body, T denotes the declared task object.

13.1.3 Task priorities

A task can be given a priority by use of the pragma

```
pragma PRIORITY (E);
```

within the task declaration, where E is a static expression of the integer subtype SYSTEM.PRIORITY. The pragma can also appear in the declarative part of a library subprogram, and takes effect only if the subprogram is used as a main program.

If no priority is given to a task, then its scheduling is implementation-dependent, except that during rendezvous with a task that has a priority it takes the task's priority. Similarly, if two tasks with different priorities rendezvous, the lower temporarily takes the higher's priority.

The pragma is largely advisory to the implementation; the only guaranteed effect is that a lower priority task does not proceed at the expense of a higher priority task when the latter is available for execution, requires no more resources, and could sensibly proceed. It has no effect on entries queued at accept statements, which are taken in strict order of arrival irrespective of priority, or on the choice of open accept alternatives in a selective wait (see below).

It is not defined whether a higher-priority task that becomes available for execution (e.g. at the expiry of a delay) preempts a lower-priority task that is executing, nor the relative scheduling of equal-priority tasks. For these implementation-dependent matters see your User's Guide.

13.1.4 Attributes of tasks

The following attributes are associated with tasks.

attribute	type	value
for a task object T or the task object designated by an access value or object T:		
T'CALLABLE	BOOLEAN	TRUE if the task is not completed, terminated, nor abnormal; FALSE otherwise

T'TERMINATED	BOOLEAN	TRUE if task T is terminated; FALSE otherwise

for a task object T, or for any object of task type T:

T'STORAGE_SIZE	*universal_integer*	number of storage units reserved for local storage for an activation of the task
T'SIZE	*universal_integer*	number of bits allocated to the task object

for a task type or single task T (see note):

T'ADDRESS	SYSTEM.ADDRESS	address of machine code of the body of task unit

for an entry E:

E'COUNT	*universal_integer*	number of calls queued on entry (note that this can change after evaluation)
E'ADDRESS	SYSTEM.ADDRESS	interrupt associated with single entry E (by a representation clause in the task declaration - see section 13.1.5)

Note. For a task object T other than a single task, T'ADDRESS is the address of the object itself.

13.1.5 Representation of tasks

Besides E'ADDRESS (section 13.1.1), the attributes STORAGE_SIZE, SIZE, and ADDRESS can (if the compiler supports it) be set for a task type T (or the type of a single task T) by means of representation clauses associated with the task declaration.

```
for T'SIZE use
   static_simple_integer_expression;
```

```
for T'STORAGE_SIZE use
  simple_integer_expression;

for T'ADDRESS use at ADDRESS_expression;
```

13.2 Task execution

The life of a task falls into five phases initiated by the events; creation, start of activation, start of execution, completion, and termination.

(1) **Creation.** A task is created on the creation of a task object by an object declaration or an allocator with a task type or composite type with a task subcomponent. After creation, it is quiescent until the end of the enclosing declarative part, or the declarative part of the package body if the declaration is in a package specification (for a declaration) or the end of the creation and initialisation of the allocated object (for an allocation). No entry calls can be made but *attributes* of the tasks can be evaluated (section 13.1.4).

If an exception occurs during the declarative part, package specification, or allocator, then any tasks created so far become terminated (see below), before the exception is handled or propogated.

If a task in this state becomes abnormal (because a task it depends on is *aborted* (section 13.3.5)), it becomes *completed* (see below).

(2) **Activation.** Activation is the elaboration of the declarative part of the task body (if there is no declarative part, activation still takes place but has no direct effect). Just before the first statement of a frame, all tasks created by declaration during the declarative part, and the package specification if the frame is a package body, start activation in parallel. Similarly, when an allocated object has been created and initialised, any tasks created during the creation start activation in parallel.

For tasks created by declarations in a package specification:

- if the package body has no statements, a single null statement is assumed
- if there is no package body, an implicit body

```
package body P is
begin
  null;
end;
```

is assumed, at the end of the declarative part of the frame enclosing the package body. If there are several such implicit package bodies, their order is undefined.

Execution of the enclosing frame continues only when all tasks are activated. If an exception occurs during the activation of one of the tasks, it becomes completed, and when all the other tasks have finished their activation or are similarly completed the exception `TASKING_ERROR` is raised in the frame (just once, no matter how many tasks fail).

(3) **Execution**. After activation, each task continues on its own way for execution of the statements of its body. The statements of the body are executed in the normal way; the effects of special tasking statements are explained in the next section.

During execution, a task may be *waiting* for several reasons:

- executing a delay statement
- waiting for an entry call to be accepted
- waiting for a timed entry call to be accepted or timed out
- waiting at an accept statement for an entry call
- waiting at a selective wait with delay alternative(s)
- waiting at a terminate alternative

In all these conditions except the last, the task eventually resumes execution, either in a rendezvous or in normal execution mode (unless it is *aborted* while waiting - see section 13.3.5). In the last case, the task waits until it becomes able to *terminate* (see below).

(4) **Completion.** Execution continues until the sequence of statements is finished, or an exception has occured with no handler in the task or the handler has finished execution. The task is then **completed**. It now waits until it can terminate.

During this phase the task can accept no further entry calls (any attempted entry call raises `TASKING_ERROR`), but dependent tasks may still be executing.

A block statement or subprogram body is also said to be completed in the same circumstances, or for a subprogram when a return statement is executed; and similarly waits for all dependent tasks to terminate before itself terminating and allowing execution of its task to proceed.

(5) **Termination**. A completed task waits until all its dependent tasks have terminated, or are waiting at open terminate alternatives; it then terminates, along with any dependent tasks not yet **terminated**. The same is true of completed block statements and subprograms.

(A **dependent** task is one declared in, or created by an allocator for a type declared in, the task body, block statement, or subprogram body.

Tasks may also be dependent on library packages – see section10.4.2 for their termination conditions.)

A terminated task plays no further part in execution of the program (though it is still interrogatable via attributes of the task object).

13.2.1 Synchronisation points

The **synchronisation points** are the points in the task's execution when it is synchronised with the execution of another task, or otherwise comes to the attention of the tasking scheduler. They include:

- end of activation
- starting activation of another task
- unconditional, conditional, or timed entry call
- start or end of accept statement
- selective wait statement
- delay statement
- exception handler
- abort statement

There may be other synchronisation points (e.g. input-output calls) – see your User's Guide.

13.3 Tasking statements

13.3.1 Rendezvous, entry calls, and accept statements

The main means of intertask communication is the **rendezvous**. This is when two executing tasks synchronise: one task `T1` (the **calling** task) executes an entry call statement

```
T2.E;              -- single entry, no parameters
T2.E(A,...);       -- single entry, with parameters

T2.E(I);           -- entry of family, no parameters
T2.E(I)(A,...);    -- entry of family, with parameters
```

for an entry `E` in the other task `T2` (the **called** task). The actual parameter associations `A` are as for a *procedure call* (section 12.1.3). For an entry of a family, the index `I` is an expression of the type of the discrete range in the entry family declaration. The task name `T2` and the index I, if there is one, are evaluated first in undefined order; CONSTRAINT_ERROR is raised if I is not in the index range. The parameter associations A are then evaluated in undefined order, as for a subprogram call.

The called task executes the corresponding accept statement:

```
accept E [(I)] [formal_part];
```

or

```
accept E [(I)] [formal_part] do
   statement;
   ...;
end [E];
```

The accept statement must be within the task body, but not within any other program unit or within any accept statement for the same entry or an entry of the same family. There should be at least one accept statement for each entry (else a call to the entry can never be accepted); there may well be more.

The entry index I is as in the entry call, and is evaluated first. The formal part is not evaluated, but it must *conform* (section 1.9) with the formal part in the corresponding entry declaration. The rendezvous consists of execution of the sequence of statements (if any) within the accept statement.

Whichever task gets there first awaits the other, or rather, as several tasks can call one entry but one task can call only one entry at once, an entry call is accepted at once if the called task is waiting at the accept statement and otherwise is queued; queued calls are processed in their order of arrival.

The rendezvous ends in the normal course of events when execution reaches the end of the accept statement, or a return statement

```
return;
```

within the accept statement (possibly nested within a block statement).

If an exception occurs during a rendezvous, and is not handled within the accept statement, then the rendezvous is abandoned. In the calling task, the exception is raised at the entry call. In the called task, the exception is raised just after the accept statement.

For the effect of *aborting* a task during a rendezvous, see section 13.3.5.

13.3.2 Selective wait statements

A **selective wait statement** allows a called task a choice of entry calls to accept or other actions. It has one of the forms

```
select
   select_alternative;
or
   ...;
end select;
```

```
select
   select_alternative;
or
   ...;
else
   statement;
   ...;
end select;
```

There are three forms of **select alternative**, each of which may be guarded by a **condition** C (a boolean expression):

(1) **accept alternative**:

```
[when C =>]
   accept_statement;
   [statement;
   ...;]
```

(2) **delay alternative**:

```
[when C =>]
   delay D;      -- D is a simple expression of type
   [statement;   -- DURATION, negative value means 0
   ...;]
```

(3) **terminate alternative**:

```
[when C =>]
   terminate;
```

A selective wait statement must always contain at least one accept alternative; the second form (with **else**) may contain nothing else. The first form may (but need not) also contain either one or more delay alternatives, or one terminate altrnative, but not both. There are thus 4 possibilities:

- one or more accept alternatives only
- one or more accept alternatives and an **else** part
- one or more accept alternatives and one or more delay alternatives
- one or more accept alternatives and one terminate alternative.

The execution is as follows. The conditions `C` are evaluated in an undefined order; this determines which alternatives are **open**, i.e. have no condition or a condition which is `TRUE`. Next the expressions `D` in any open delay alternatives and the entry indices `I` in any open accept alternatives are evaluated in an undefined order. Finally an open alternative or the **else** part is selected as follows and executed.

(1) If there is at least one open accept alternative which is *selectable*, i.e. has an entry call queued, one is chosen arbitrarily and the accept statement and subsequent statements are executed.

(2) If there is no open selectable accept alternative but there is at least one open delay alternative, then the task waits for the period of time of the shortest open delay alternative (which may be zero) and if no open accept alternative has become selectable by then that delay alternative is chosen and its sequence of statements is executed. If there are several open delay alternatives with the same delay then one is chosen arbitrarily.

(3) If there is no open selectable accept alternative but there is an open terminate alternative, and the task is able to terminate (see above), then the terminate alternative is chosen: the task terminates.

(4) If there is no open selectable accept alternative but there is an **else** part, then the sequence of statements in the **else** part is executed.

(5) If there are open accept alternatives but none are selectable, and there is no open delay or terminate alternative or else part, then the task waits for one of the open accept alternatives to become selectable and chooses the first one to do so (if several do so at the same time one is chosen arbitrarily).

(6) If there are no open alternatives and no **else** part, `PROGRAM_ERROR` is raised.

13.3.3 *Conditional and timed entry calls*

An unconditional entry call is queued indefinitely if it cannot be accepted at once. *Conditional* and *timed* entry calls allow other actions to be taken if that happens.

A **conditional entry call** has the form

```
select
   entry_call_statement;
   [statement;
   ...;]
else
   statement;
   ...;
end select;
```

If the entry call can be accepted at once it is; and after the rendezvous the following statements, if any, are executed. Otherwise the rendezvous is abandoned and the statements after the **else** are executed instead.

A **timed entry call** has one of the forms

```
select
    entry_call_statement;
   [statement;
    ...;]
   delay D;      -- D is a simple expression of type DURATION
   [statement;   -- negative value means 0.
    ...;]
end select;
```

Here the entry call is cancelled, and the second sequence of statements is executed, if the called task cannot accept the call immediately or within the specified delay D.

In either case TASKING_ERROR is raised (in the calling task) if the called task is completed or abnormal, or becomes so before the entry call is accepted or cancelled.

13.3.4 *Time*

Time is represented in two ways: clock time (plus calendar date) by the private type CALENDAR.TIME (section 16.2.1), and duration (in seconds) by the implementation-defined fixed point type STANDARD.DURATION. The accuracy and range of DURATION are implementation-defined, but must be no worse respectively than a small of 0.02 (i.e. 20 milliseconds) and a range of -86400 to 86400 (i.e. ±24 hours). Real-time processors can be expected to provide greater accuracy; the Reference Manual recommends at least 0.0005 (50 microseconds) wherever possible. Consult your User's Guide.

A simple delay is caused by a **delay statement**

```
delay D;
```

where the simple expression D is of type DURATION. The task executing the delay statement is suspended for *at least* the time given by the value of the expression (a negative value is taken as zero). The delay may be greater than D either because of timing inaccuracies, or because of preemption by a higher-priority task. Precautions must be taken if required against these possibilities.

13.3.5 Task abortion

A task can **abort** another task or itself by an **abort statement**

```
abort T,...;
```

The task names T are evaluated in an undefined order. The tasks T, and any tasks depending on them, then become **abnormal** (unless already terminated) and are unable to accept any further entry calls. For any waiting entry calls on T, TASKING_ERROR is raised at the point of call, at some time between the called task's becoming abnormal and its completion.

What happens next to each named or dependent task depends on its state; the order in which these effects occur among the tasks involved is undefined.

(1) The task T has not yet finished (or not yet started) activation: T is completed; there is no effect on activating task.

(2) The task T is waiting at entry call: T is completed and removed from entry queue; there is no other effect on the called task.

(3) The task T is waiting at accept statement, selective wait, timed entry call, or delay statement: T is completed.

(4) The task T is the calling task in a rendezvous: T is completed

at some time no later than the next *synchronisation point* (this must be before the end of the rendezvous – see section 13.3.1); the rendezvous finishes normally, after which the task `T` is terminated. There is no effect on the called task.

(5) The task `T` is the called task in a rendezvous: `TASKING_ERROR` is raised in the calling task, and the task `T` is completed at some time no later than the next *synchronisation point* of `T` (section 13.2.1).

(6) The task `T` is in any other executing state: `T` is completed no later than the next synchronisation point .

(7) Completed or terminated: no effect.

In cases (1), (2), and (3) the task executing the abort statement waits for the effect to take place before continuing execution.

Great care should be taken with abort statements, and they should be used only in the last resort. The exact effects in some situations are not well defined, e.g. when the aborted task is itself part way through an abort statement.

13.4 Shared variables

Besides rendezvous, tasks can communicate via **shared variables**, i.e. variables accessible to both tasks. If this is done it is up to the programmer to ensure that inconsistent results cannot be obtained.

In particular the program is erroneous if, for a scalar or access shared variable `V`, between two successive *synchronisation points* of a task `T` (section 13.2.1) either `T` reads `V` and another task updates `V`, or `T` updates `V` and another task makes any access (read or update) to `V`. `V` is restricted to scalar or access so that `T1` and `T2` can access different components of a composite variable without harm; though this may not be possible if the components are packed by pragma `PACK` or a representation clause (sections 6.1.7, 6.2.11). Scalar or access subcomponents of composite variables are considered as variables and are covered by this rule. This rule allows a copy of a variable to be held in a register between synchronisation points.

A program is also erroneous if it relies on the relative order of accesses to shared variables in two tasks `T1` and `T2` except at one of the following points of mutual synchronisation

- the start or end of a rendezvous between `T1` and `T2`
- the start or end of `T1`'s activation of `T2` (or vice versa).

It is possible to force every access to a shared scalar or access variable V to be performed indivisibly and effectively by the pragma

```
pragma SHARED (V);
```

V must be the identifier of a declared variable; there are likely to be further implementation-dependent restrictions. The pragma must be in the same package specification or declarative part as, and after, the declaration of V, and with no uses of V (except in an address clause) in betweeen.

The effect is that the value of the variable as read is always as set by the last update, so every access to the variable acts as a synchronisation point for the accessing task. The relative order of accesses in different tasks is still undefined.

14 Generic Units

Generic units are templates for the generation of subprograms and packages. They can be parameterised by *generic formal parameters* of various kinds, which are replaced by *generic actual parameters* when the actual subprograms and packages are generated. The process of generating an instance of a generic unit is called *instantiation*.

14.1 Generic declarations

A generic unit is declared in two parts, a *generic specification* and a *generic body*; unlike a (nongeneric) subprogram, there is no option of combining the specification and body of a generic subprogram. A **generic specification** is presented in a **generic declaration** (see below); the generic specification is the generic declaration without the terminating semicolon. A **generic body** is exactly the same as a nongeneric subprogram or package body, except that it may contain uses of the generic formal parameters.

A generic subprogram or package declaration has the form of a nongeneric subprogram or package declaration preceded by the reserved word **generic** and an optional sequence of *generic parameter declarations*:

```
generic
   [generic_parameter_declaration;
   ...;]
procedure G [(A; ...)];

generic
   [generic_parameter_declaration;
   ...;]
function G [(A; ...)] return T;
-- G must be an identifier, not an operator symbol
```

```
generic
   [generic_parameter_declaration;
   ...;]
package G is
   [declarative_item;
   ...;]
   [private
   declarative_item
   ...;]
end [G];
```

Within the generic unit, the unit identifier G denotes the current instance of the generic unit. Outside, it denotes the generic unit itself.

Elaborating a generic declaration or body has no effect, other than to make the generic unit instantiatable. Any expressions in the generic declaration are evaluated either when the generic unit is instantiated (default values for generic formal parameters) or when the instance is called or elaborated.

14.2 Generic instantiation

An instance of a generic unit G is created by a **generic instantiation**, with one of 3 forms depending on the kind of unit.

```
procedure I is new G [([F =>] A, ... )];

function I is new G [([F =>] A, ... )];

package I is new G [([F =>] A, ... )];
```

where the F are the generic formal parameters and the A are the generic actual parameters. The rules for the *associations* are as described in section 1.7; named associations are not allowed for formal parameters with the same name (this can only occur for overloaded subprograms).

Allowable generic actual parameters are described below for each kind of generic formal parameter.

The effect of elaborating the instantiation is to create an instance I of the generic unit, i.e. a copy I of the nongeneric unit specification and the generic body. Within the instance, the generic formal parameters and associated names denote actual entities as follows.

generic name:	meaning in instance:
generic unit name G	this instance I
generic formal parameter F	corresponding generic actual parameter A
discriminant D of generic formal type	corresponding discriminant of generic actual type
formal parameter of generic formal subprogram	corresponding formal parameter of generic actual subprogram

Note that recursive instantiation is not allowed: if a generic unit A includes an instantiation of a generic unit B, then that instance of B must not include an instance of A, directly or indirectly.

14.3 Generic formal parameters

There are 3 kinds of **generic formal parameter**: objects, types, and subprograms. Each must be replaced by a **generic actual parameter** denoting an entity of the same kind on instantiation. The generic parameter declarations and rules for instantiation are given below.

The identifiers or operator symbols of generic formal parameters must all be different, except that *overloaded* generic formal subprograms are allowed (section 12.3). They can be used in later generic formal parameters, in default expressions or (for generic formal types) as type marks.

14.3.1 Generic formal objects

The generic parameter declaration has one of the forms

```
I, ... : [in] T [:=E];

I, ... : in out T;
```

A multiple declaration with more than one identifier is treated as explained in section 1.8. T is a type mark giving the type T'BASE of the object.

In the first form, with mode **in** (the default), the corresponding generic actual parameter must be an expression of type T'BASE, or may be omitted if a default expression E is given. The generic formal parameter I is a constant with the value and subtype of the actual parameter, or the value of the default expression E and subtype given by the type mark T if there is no actual parameter.

In the second form, with mode **in out**, the corresponding generic actual parameter must be a variable of type T'BASE. No default expression is allowed. The generic formal parameter I denotes the same variable, as with a *renaming declaration* (section 3.2.5).

14.3.2 Generic formal types

There are seven forms of generic type declaration, according to the class of the type. In each case the allowed actual parameter is a type mark of a type or subtype of the same class, with further restrictions as described below. The unspecified part of the generic type is indicated by the symbol <>, pronounced *box*. The appropriate *basic operations* and *predefined operators* for the class of types are implicitly declared at the generic formal type declaration. On instantiation, these are converted to the corresponding basic operations and predefined operators for the actual types (even if a predefined operator has been redefined for the actual type).

T and C are type marks; the D are discriminant specifications (default values for discriminants are not allowed).

(1) Discrete types:

```
type I is (<>);
```

Generic actual type: any discrete (i.e. integer or enumeration) type or subtype.

(2) Integer types:

```
type I is range <>;
```

Generic actual type: any integer type or subtype.

(3) Floating-point types:

```
type I is digits <>;
```

Generic actual type: any floating-point type or subtype.

(4) Fixed-point types:

```
type I is delta <>;
```

Generic actual type: any fixed-point type or subtype.

(5) Array types:

```
type I is array (T range <>, ...) of C;
-- unconstrained

type I is array (T, ...) of C;
-- constrained
```

Generic actual type: any array type or unconstrained array subtype (first form) or constrained array subtype (second form), with the same dimensionality, the same index types `T'BASE` and component type `C'BASE`; and if `C` is a constrained or unconstrained record, array, or access type, the actual component subtype must be constrained or unconstrained respectively.

(6) Access types:

```
type I is access T;
```

Generic actual type: an access type or subtype with the same designated type `T'BASE`; and if `T` is a constrained or unconstrained record, array, or access type, the actual designated subtype must be constrained or unconstrained respectively.

(7) Private types:

```
type I is private;
-- nonlimited type, no discriminants

type I is limited private;
-- limited type, no discriminants

type I (D, ... : T; ... ) is private;
-- nonlimited type with discriminants
```

```
type I (D,... : T; ... ) is limited
private;        -- limited type with discriminants
```

Generic actual type: any type or subtype satisfying the following.

- Formal type nonlimited: actual type must be nonlimited.
- Formal type limited: actual type may be limited or nonlimited.
- Formal type has discriminants: actual type must have the same number and types of discriminants, and actual subtype must be unconstrained.
- Formal type has no discriminants: actual type may have any number of discriminants, or none; actual subtype may be constrained or unconstrained.

14.3.3 Generic formal subprograms

There are two forms of generic subprogram parameter declaration, corresponding to procedures and functions:

```
with procedure P [(I, ...: [mode] T; ...)]
[is default];

with function F [(I, ...: [mode] T; ...)]
return R [is default];
```

The subprogram designator P or F, and parameter and result types T and R and parameter modes follow the same rules as for nongeneric subprogram declarations (sections 12.1.1, 12.2.1).

The actual subprogram parameter can be any subprogram, enumeration literal, or entry provided that they *match,* i.e. have the same number, modes, and types of parameters, and are both procedures or both functions with the same result type. An enumeration literal counts as a parameterless function returning an enumeration value. An entry counts as a procedure with the same formal parameters.

The actual subprogram parameter can be defaulted. The *default*, if present, is one of

(1) the name of a subprogram, enumeration literal, or entry that matches the formal subprogram (as explained above)

(2) the box <>, meaning the unique such matching subprogram, enumeration literal, or entry, with the same designator, directly visible at the instantiation (there must be just one such).

The actual subprogram (explicitly provided or defaulted) need not have the same formal parameter names and default expressions as the generic formal subprogram. The generic formal parameter declaration acts similarly to a renaming declaration: the formal parameter names and any default expressions override those of the actual subprogram.

The subtypes of the formal parameters of the actual subprogram (explicitly provided or defaulted) need not have the same as for the generic formal subprogram. The constraints implied by the latter are ignored: the constraints applying to the formal parameters of the generic formal subprogram are those in this case the formal parameters of the subprogram are constrained by the subtypes of the actual subprogram's formal parameters.

15 Input and Output

The Ada language provides **input-output** facilities defined by predifined packages using the normal features of the language. These package specifications are given below with added comments describing the facilities provided. *Low level* input-output (for physical devices) is supported by the implementation-dependent package LOW_LEVEL_IO, and is independent of the remaining (high level) input-output system. *Unformatted* (binary) input-output is supported by two generic packages, one for *direct access* files (DIRECT_IO) and one for *sequential* files (SEQUENTIAL_IO); in each case the generic package is instantiated with the actual type to be mapped on to an element of the file. *Formatted* (textual, human-readable) input-output is supported by a package TEXT_IO which, besides general housekeeping facilities and input-output procedures for CHARACTER and STRING objects, contains generic packages (to be instantiated with the actual element type) for input-output of integer, floating-point, fixed-point, and enumeration types.

The input-output facilities described here are particular to Ada programs; it may be difficult or impossible to use them to read files created by programs written in other languages, or *vice versa*.

15.1 Low level input-output

Low level input-output means the monitoring and control of physical devices by the program. Any such facilities that are provided are supported by the predefined package LOW_LEVEL_IO, which provides overloaded procedures RECEIVE_CONTROL (for input) and SEND_CONTROL (for output) for all available devices and input-output data types. Full information should be in your User's Guide.

```
package LOW_LEVEL_IO is
   -- declarations of the possible types for DEVICE and DATA;
   -- declarations of overloaded procedures for these types;
   procedure SEND_CONTROL
      (DEVICE : device_type;
       DATA   : in out data_type);
   procedure RECEIVE_CONTROL
      (DEVICE : device_type;
       DATA   : in out data_type);
end LOW_LEVEL_IO;
```

15.2 Files

A distinction is drawn between **external files**, which are under the control of the environment, and (internal) **files**, which are objects within the Ada program representing external files.

All that is assumed about external files is that they can be identified by means of names in the form of strings; these names are given to the CREATE and OPEN procedures that associate a file with an external file, and are not referred to thereafter. Provision is also made for implementation-dependent information associated with the external file in the *form* string.

Whether more than one file can be associated with an external file, and if so how many and the exact effect, are implementation-dependent.

The types of internal files are the limited private types FILE_TYPE declared in instantiations of DIRECT_IO and SEQUENTIAL_IO and in TEXT_IO. As the types are limited, assignment of file objects is not possible, and the only way a file object can acquire a value is as a parameter to one of the input-output procedures OPEN or CREATE.

A file is either **open** or **closed**. If it is open, it has one of the **modes** IN_FILE, OUT_FILE, and (for direct files only) INOUT_FILE: respectively for reading only, for writing only, and for both reading and writing.

15.3 Input-output exceptions

There are seven exceptions that can be raised by the input-output subprograms. They each cover a broad class of erroneous situations, described below; for more details see the descriptions of the various input-output subprograms. The exceptions are declared in the environment package IO_EXCEPTIONS.

```
package IO_EXCEPTIONS is

   STATUS_ERROR : exception
   -- attempt to access or close a closed file;
   -- attempt to open an open file

   MODE_ERROR : exception;
   -- attempt to read from or test for end of an out file;
   -- attempt to write to an in file;
   -- attempt to set or read line or page length of an in file;
   -- attempt to set an out file as standard input, or vice versa.

   NAME_ERROR : exception;
   -- attempt to create or open an external file with an invalid
   -- NAME parameter.

   USE_ERROR : exception;
   -- attempt to perform an operation not supported by the
   -- external file, including invalid FORM parameter.

   DEVICE_ERROR : exception;
   -- system malfunction.

   END_ERROR : exception;
   -- attempt to read past the end of a file.

   DATA_ERROR : exception;
   -- attempt to read a value which cannot be interpreted as of
   -- the required type.

   LAYOUT_ERROR : exception;
   -- (TEXT_IO) column, line, or page number out of range
   -- attempt to set column number beyond maximum line
   -- length, or line number beyond maximum page length;
   -- attempt to write too many characters to a string.

end IO_EXCEPTIONS;
```

15.4 Sequential input-output

A **sequential** external file is regarded as a sequence of elements which can be written or read only in sequence from the beginning. The available operations are described below as comments on the specification of the generic package SEQUENTIAL_IO.

```
with IO_EXCEPTIONS;
generic
  type ELEMENT TYPE is private;
package SEQUENTIAL_IO is

  type FILE_TYPE is limited private;
  type FILE_MODE is (IN_FILE, OUT_FILE);

-- 15.4.1 File management

  procedure CREATE (FILE: in out FILE_TYPE;
                    MODE: in FILE_MODE := OUT_FILE;
                    NAME: in STRING := "";
                    FORM: in STRING := "");
  -- creates a new external sequential file with name NAME and
  -- form FORM, and associates it with internal file FILE, which
  -- it leaves open in mode MODE. Null string for NAME means
  -- temporary external file: null string for FORM means system
  -- defaults.
  -- Exceptions raised:
  --   STATUS_ERROR if the file FILE is already open;
  --   NAME_ERROR if the name NAME is invalid;
  --   USE_ERROR if operation is impossible for other reasons.

  procedure OPEN (FILE: in out FILE_TYPE;
                  MODE: in FILE_MODE;
                  NAME: in STRING;
                  FORM: in STRING := "");
  -- Locates existing external sequential file NAME with form
  -- FORM (system defaults if null), and associates it with
  -- internal file FILE, which it leaves open in mode MODE.
  -- Exceptions raised:
  --   STATUS_ERROR if file FILE is already open;
  --   NAME_ERROR if name NAME is invalid or not the name
  --   of an existing external file;
  --   USE_ERROR if operation is impossible for other reasons.
```

```
procedure CLOSE (FILE: in out FILE_TYPE);
-- Closes the file FILE and disassociates it from the associated
-- external file.
-- Exceptions if raised:
--   STATUS_ERROR if file FILE is closed.

procedure DELETE (FILE: in out FILE_TYPE);
-- Closes file FILE and deletes its associated external file.
-- Exceptions raised
--   STATUS_ERROR if file FILE is closed;
--   USE_ERROR if operation is impossible for other reasons.

procedure RESET (FILE: in out FILE_TYPE:
                 MODE: in FILE_MODE);
procedure RESET (FILE: in out FILE_TYPE);
-- Resets file FILE to the beginning: sets access mode to MODE,
-- if given, otherwise leaves it as it is.
-- Exceptions raised:
--   STATUS_ERROR if file FILE is closed;
--   USE_ERROR if operation is impossible for other reasons.

function MODE (FILE: in FILE_TYPE)
 return FILE_MODE;
-- Returns mode of file FILE.
-- Exceptions raised:
--   STATUS_ERROR if file FILE is closed.

function NAME (FILE: in FILE_TYPE)
 return STRING;
-- Returns full name of external file associated with file FILE.
-- Exceptions raised:
--   STATUS_ERROR if file FILE is closed.

function FORM (FILE: in FILE_TYPE)
 return STRING;
-- Returns full form string for external file associated with file
-- FILE.
-- Exceptions raised:
--   STATUS_ERROR if file FILE is closed.
```

```
    function IS_OPEN (FILE: in FILE_TYPE)
     return BOOLEAN;
    -- Returns TRUE if file FILE is open and FALSE if not.
    -- Exceptions raised: none.

--  15.4.2  Input and output operations

    procedure READ (FILE: in FILE_TYPE;
                    ITEM: out ELEMENT_TYPE);
    -- Mode: IN_FILE.
    -- Returns next element from file FILE in ITEM.
    -- Exceptions raised:
    --   MODE_ERROR if file FILE is not open in mode IN_FILE
    --   END_ERROR if there is no next element
    --   DATA_ERROR if next element is invalid (optional).

    procedure WRITE (FILE: in FILE_TYPE;
                     ITEM: in ELEMEMT_TYPE);
    -- Mode: OUT_FILE.
    -- Writes element ITEM as next element of file FILE.
    -- Exceptions raised:
    --   MODE_ERROR if file FILE is not open in mode OUT_FILE
    --   USE_ERROR if the external file is full.

    function END_OF_FILE (FILE: in FILE_TYPE)
    return BOOLEAN;
    -- Mode: IN_FILE.
    -- Returns TRUE if end of file FILE has been reached
    -- (no more elements can be read), FALSE otherwise.
    -- Exceptions raised:
    --   MODE_ERROR if file FILE is not open in mode IN_FILE.

--  15.4.3  Exceptions

    STATUS_ERROR : exception renames
      IO_EXCEPTIONS.STATUS_ERROR;
    MODE_ERROR   : exception renames
      IO_EXCEPTIONS.MODE_ERROR;
    NAME_ERROR   : exception renames
      IO_EXCEPTIONS.NAME_ERROR;
    USE_ERROR    : exception renames
      IO_EXCEPTIONS.USE_ERROR;
    DEVICE_ERROR : exception renames
```

```
        IO_EXCEPTIONS.DEVICE ERROR;
    END_ERROR      : exception renames
        IO_EXCEPTIONS.END_ERROR;
    DATA_ERROR     : exception renames
        IO_EXCEPTIONS.DATE_ERROR;
private
    -- implementation-dependent
end SEQUENTIAL_IO;
```

15.5 Direct input-output

A **direct** external file is regarded as a sequence of elements, **indexed** sequentially from 1, which can be written or read either in sequence from any point, or directly by specifying the index. The number of elements in the external file is its **current size**; it is also (if nonzero) the index of the last element of the file. An open direct file has a **current index** associated with the internal file; this is the index of the next element to be written or read sequentially. The available operations are described below as comments on the specification of the generic package DIRECT_IO.

```
with IO_EXCEPTIONS;
generic
    type ELEMENT_TYPE is private;
package DIRECT_IO is

    type FILE_TYPE is limited private;
    type FILE_MODE is (IN_FILE, INOUT_FILE,
                       OUT_FILE);

    type COUNT is range
         0..implementation defined;
    -- Type COUNT is used for sizes of direct external files
    subtype POSITIVE_COUNT is COUNT range
            1..COUNT'LAST;
    -- Subtype POSITIVE_COUNT is used for index values of
    -- direct files.
```

```
-- 15.5.1 File management

   procedure CREATE (FILE: in out FILE_TYPE;
                     MODE: in FILE_MODE :=
                           INOUT_FILE;
                     NAME: in STRING := "";
                     FORM: in STRING := "");
   -- Creates a new external direct file with name NAME, form
   -- FORM, and implementation-dependent size, and associates it
   -- with internal file FILE, which it leaves open in mode MODE.
   -- Null string for NAME means temporary external file; null
   -- string for FORM means system defaults.
   -- Exceptions raised:
   --   STATUS_ERROR if file FILE is already open
   --   NAME_ERROR if NAME is invalid
   --   USE_ERROR if operation is impossible for other reasons.

   procedure OPEN (FILE: in out FILE_TYPE;
                   MODE: in FILE_MODE;
                   NAME: in STRING;
                   FORM: in STRING := "");

   -- Locates the (existing) external direct file NAME with form
   -- FORM (system defaults if null), and associates it with
   -- internal file FILE, which it leaves open in mode MODE.
   -- Exceptions raised:
   --   STATUS_ERROR if file NAME is already open;
   --   NAME_ERROR if the name NAME is invalid or does not
   --   identify an existing external file with form FORM;
   --   USE_ERROR if operation is impossible for other reasons.

   procedure CLOSE (FILE: in out FILE_TYPE);
   -- Closes file FILE and disassociates it from its associated
   -- external file.
   -- Exceptions raised:
   --   STATUS_ERROR if file FILE is not open.

   procedure DELETE (FILE: in out FILE_TYPE);
   -- Closes file FILE and deletes its associated external file.
   -- Exceptions raised:
   --   STATUS_ERROR if file FILE is not open
   --   USE_ERROR if operation is impossible for other reasons.
```

```
procedure RESET (FILE: in out FILE_TYPE;
                 MODE: in FILE_MODE);
procedure RESET (FILE: in out FILE_TYPE);
-- Resets file FILE to the beginning (current index is 1);
-- sets mode to MODE, if given, otherwise leaves it as it is.
-- Exceptions raised:
--   STATUS_ERROR if file FILE is not open;
--   USE_ERROR if operation is impossible for other reasons.

function MODE (FILE: in FILE_TYPE)
 return FILE_MODE;
-- Returns mode of file FILE.
-- Exceptions raised:
--   STATUS_ERROR if file FILE is closed.

function NAME(FILE: in FILE_TYPE)
 return STRING;
-- Returns full name of external file associated with file FILE.
-- Exceptions raised:
--    STATUS_ERROR if file FILE is closed.

function FORM (FILE: in FILE_TYPE)
 return STRING;
-- Returns full form string for external file associated with file
-- FILE.
-- Exceptions raised:
--   STATUS_ERROR if file FILE is closed.

function IS_OPEN (FILE: in FILE_TYPE)
 return BOOLEAN;
-- Returns TRUE if file FILE is open and FALSE if closed.
-- Exceptions raised: none.
```

-- *15.5.2 Input and output operations*

```
procedure READ (FILE: in FILE_TYPE;
                ITEM: out ELEMENT_TYPE;
                FROM: POSITIVE_COUNT);
procedure READ (FILE: out FILE_TYPE);
                ITEM: out ELEMENT_TYPE);
-- Mode: IN_FILE or INOUT_FILE.
-- Sets current index of file FILE to FORM, if given, otherwise
-- leaves it unchanged; then reads the element at that position to
```

```
-- ITEM and increases the current index by 1.
-- Exceptions raised:
--   MODE_ERROR if file FILE is not open in mode IN_FILE
--   or INOUT_FILE.
--   END_ERROR if index value to be used is beyond size of file.
--   DATA_ERROR if element read is invalid (optional - see
--   your User's Guide).

procedure WRITE (FILE: in FILE_TYPE;
                 ITEM: in ELEMENT_TYPE;
                 TO  : in POSITIVE_COUNT);
procedure WRITE (FILE: in FILE_TYPE;
                 ITEM: in ELEMENT_TYPE);
-- Mode: INOUT_FILE or OUT_FILE.
-- Sets current index of file FILE to TO, if given, otherwise
-- leaves it unchanged; writes value of ITEM to element at that
-- position.
-- Exceptions raised:
--   MODE_ERROR if file FILE is not open in mode
--   INOUT_FILE or OUT_FILE.
--   END_ERROR if index value to be used is beyond size of file.

procedure SET_INDEX(FILE: in FILE_TYPE;
                    TO  : in POSITIVE_COUNT);
-- Mode: any.
-- Sets current index of file FILE to TO.
-- Exceptions raised: none.

function INDEX (FILE: in FILE_TYPE)
 return POSITIVE_COUNT;
-- Mode: any.
-- Returns current index of file FILE.
   -- Exceptions raised: none.

function SIZE (FILE: in FILE_TYPE)
 return COUNT;
-- Mode: any.
-- Returns size of external file associated with file FILE.
-- Exceptions raised: none.
```

```
function END_OF_FILE (FILE : in FILE_TYPE)
 return BOOLEAN;
-- Mode: IN_FILE or INOUT_FILE.
-- Returns TRUE if current index of file FILE is greater than
-- size of associated external file, otherwise FALSE.
-- Exceptions raised:
--   MODE_ERROR if file FILE is not open in mode IN_FILE
--   or INOUT_FILE.
```

```
-- 15.5.3 Exceptions

   STATUS_ERROR : exception renames
     IO_EXCEPTIONS.STATUS_ERROR;
   MODE_ERROR   : exception renames
     IO_EXCEPTIONS.MODE_ERROR;
   NAME_ERROR   : exception renames
     IO_EXCEPTIONS.NAME_ERROR;
   USE_ERROR    : exception renames
     IO_EXCEPTIONS.USE_ERROR;
   DEVICE_ERROR : exception renames
     IO_EXCEPTIONS.DEVICE_ERROR;
   END_ERROR    : exception renames
     IO_EXCEPTIONS.END_ERROR;
   DATA_ERROR   : exception renames
     IO_EXCEPTIONS.DATA_ERROR;

private
   -- implementation-dependent
end DIRECT_IO;
```

16 Text Input-Output

A **text file** is regarded as a sequence of characters accessed sequentially, and grouped into *lines*, themselves grouped into *pages*. A **line** may contains any number of characters from 0 to a limit, or unlimited; similarly a **page** may contain any number of lines from 0 to a limit, or unlimited (within an implementation-dependent limit). These limits may be set by the program for an output file.

Text input-output is supported by a standard (non-generic) package `TEXT_IO`. The usual file management facilities are provided. There are also facilities for manipulating lines and pages; these are described in terms of a conceptual *pointer* associated with each open text file that points to the next character to be read or written, or (in an input file) to the end of a line or of the file. Character positions in a line (called **columns**), lines in a page, and pages in a file, are all numbered from 1: the numbers associated with the conceptual ponter are called the **current column number**, the **current line number**, and the **current page number**, respectively. The end of line has column number 1 more than the length of the line.

The standard package `TEXT_IO` supports reading and writing operations (via subprograms called `GET` and `PUT` respectively) for all scalar types: by inner generic packages to be instantiated for the particular type or subtype required for integer, floating-point, fixed-point, and enumeration types, and by special procedures for the predefined enumeration type `CHARACTER`.

The page, line, and column control subprograms and the `GET` and subprograms are all provided in 2 overloaded forms: with and without a specific file parameter. The default file is either the current default input file or the *current default output file,* according to the mode required. Procedures are provided to set these defaults. At the start of the program they are set to 2 implementation-defined files called *standard-input* and *standard-output* : these are opened at the start of the program and cannot thereafter be closed, reset, or deleted. The mapping of standard input and output should be defined in the User's Guide; for an online system they are usually both mapped to the user's terminal.

The subprograms are described below by comments in the specification of the standard package `TEXT_IO`.

```
with IO_EXCEPTIONS;
package TEXT_IO is

   type FILE_TYPE is limited private;
   type FILE_MODE is (IN_FILE, OUT_FILE);

   type COUNT is range
     0..implementation-defined;
   subtype POSITIVE_COUNT is COUNT range
     1..COUNT'LAST;
   UNBOUNDED : constant COUNT := 0;
   -- COUNT is used for line and page lengths; the value 0
   -- (UNBOUNDED) has the conventional meaning of unbounded
   -- length.
   -- Subtype POSITIVE_COUNT is used for column, line, and
   -- page numbers, all starting at 1.

   subtype field is INTEGER range
     0..implementation-defined;
   -- The range of field widths available for reading and writing
   -- single items.

   subtype NUMBER_BASE is INTEGER range 2..16;
   -- The range of bases available for numeric input-output.
```

-- **16.1 File management**

```
   procedure CREATE (FILE: in out FILE_TYPE;
                     MODE: in FILE_MODE := OUT_FILE;
                     NAME: in STRING := "";
                     FORM: in STRING := "");
   -- Creates a new external file with name NAME and form FORM,
   -- and associates it with internal file FILE, which it leaves
   -- open in mode MODE. Null string for NAME means temporary
   -- external file; null string for FORM means system defaults.
   -- Exceptions raised:
   --   STATUS_ERROR if file FILE is already open
   --   NAME_ERROR if NAME is not a valid file name
   --   USE_ERROR if operation is impossible for other reasons.
```

```
procedure OPEN (FILE: in out FILE_TYPE;
                MODE: in FILE_MODE ;
                NAME: in STRING;
                FORM: in STRING := "");
-- Locates the existing external file NAME with form FORM
-- (system defaults if null), and associates it with internal file
-- FILE, which it leaves open in mode MODE.
-- Exceptions raised:
--   STATUS_ERROR if file FILE is already open;
--   NAME_ERROR if NAME is invalid or does not identify an
--    existing file with form FORM;
--   USE_ERROR if operation is impossible for other reasons.

procedure CLOSE (FILE: in out FILE_TYPE);
-- Closes file FILE and disassociates it from its associated
-- external file.
-- Exceptions raised:
--   STATUS_ERROR if the file FILE is already closed.

procedure DELETE (FILE: in out FILE_TYPE);
-- Closes file FILE and deletes its associated external file.
-- Exceptions raised:
--   STATUS_ERROR if file FILE is already closed;
--   USE_ERROR if operation is impossible for other reasons.

procedure RESET (FILE: in out FILE_TYPE
                 MODE: in FILE_TYPE);
procedure RESET (FILE: in out FILE_TYPE);
-- Resets file FILE; sets its mode to MODE, if given, otherwise
-- leaves it as it is.
-- Exceptions raised:
--   STATUS_ERROR if file FILE is already closed;
--   USE_ERROR if operation is impossible for other reasons.

function MODE (FILE: in out FILE_TYPE)
 return FILE_MODE;
-- Returns the mode of file FILE.
-- Exceptions raised:
-- STATUS_ERROR if file FILE is closed.
```

```
function NAME (FILE: in out FILE_TYPE)
 return STRING;
-- Returns full name of external file associated with file FILE.
-- Exceptions raised:
-- STATUS_ERROR if file FILE is already closed.

function FORM (FILE: in out FILE_TYPE)
 return STRING;
-- Returns full form string for external file associated with
-- file FILE.
-- Exceptions raised:
--   STATUS_ERROR if file FILE is already closed.

function IS_OPEN (FILE: in out FILE_TYPE)
 return BOOLEAN;
-- Returns TRUE if file FILE is open and FALSE if closed.
-- Exceptions raised: none.
```

-- **16.2 Control of default input and output files**

```
procedure SET_INPUT (FILE: in FILE_TYPE);
-- Sets the current input file to be file FILE.
-- Exceptions raised:
--   STATUS_ERROR if file FILE is closed;
--   MODE_ERROR if file FILE is open but its mode is not
--   IN_FILE.

procedure SET_OUTPUT (FILE: in FILE_TYPE);
-- Sets the current output file to be file FILE.
-- Exceptions raised:
--   STATUS_ERROR if file FILE is closed;
--   MODE_ERROR if file FILE is open but its mode is not
--   OUT_FILE;

function STANDARD_INPUT return FILE_TYPE;
-- Returns the identity of the standard input file.
-- Exceptions raised: none.

function STANDARD_OUTPUT return FILE_TYPE;
-- Returns the identity of the standard output file.
-- Exceptions raised: none.
```

```
function CURRENT_INPUT return FILE_TYPE;
-- Returns the identity of the current input file.
-- Exceptions raised: none.


function CURRENT_OUTPUT return FILE_TYPE;
-- Returns the identity of the current output file.
-- Exceptions raised: none.

-- Most of the following subprograms have two forms, with and
-- without a FILE_TYPE parameter FILE. The operation is done
-- on the file FILE or the current default input or output file
-- (according to mode) respectively.
```

-- 16.3 Specification of line and page lengths

```
procedure SET_LINE (FILE: in FILE_TYPE
                    TO  : in COUNT);
procedure SET_LINE (FILE: in FILE_TYPE);
-- Mode: OUT_FILE.
-- Sets maximum line length to TO (0 means unbounded).
-- Exceptions raised:
--   STATUS_ERROR if file FILE is closed;
--   MODE_ERROR if file is open but not in mode OUT_FILE;
--   USE_ERROR if specified line length TO is invalid for
--   associated external file.

procedure SET_PAGE (FILE: in FILE_TYPE
                    TO  : in COUNT);
procedure SET_PAGE (FILE: in FILE_TYPE);
-- Mode: OUT_FILE.
-- Sets maximum page length to TO (0 means unbounded).
-- Exceptions raised:
--   STATUS_ERROR if file FILE is closed;
--   MODE_ERROR if file is open but not in mode OUT_FILE;
--   USE_ERROR if specified page length TO is invalid for
--   associated external file.
```

```
function  LINE_LENGTH (FILE: in FILE_TYPE)
 return COUNT;
function LINE_LENGTH return COUNT;
-- Mode: OUT_FILE.
-- Returns maximum line length;  0 means unbounded.
-- Exceptions raised:
--   STATUS_ERROR if file is closed;
--   MODE_ERROR if file is open but not in mode OUT_FILE.

function PAGE_LENGTH (FILE: in FILE_TYPE)
 return COUNT;
function PAGE_LENGTH return COUNT;
-- Mode: OUT_FILE.
-- Returns maximum page length;  0 means unbounded.
-- Exceptions raised:
--   STATUS_ERROR if file is closed;
--   MODE_ERROR if file is open but not in mode OUT_FILE.
```

-- **16.4 Column, line, and page control**

```
  procedure NEW_LINE (FILE: in FILE_TYPE;
                      SPACING: in POSITIVE_COUNT := 1);
  procedure NEW_LINE (SPACING:
                               in POSITIVE_COUNT := 1);
-- Mode: OUT_FILE;
-- The following action is performed SPACING times:
--   Terminate current line, and current page if full; move pointer
--   to the column 1 of next line.
-- Exceptions raised:
--   STATUS_ERROR if file is closed;
--   MODE_ERROR if file is open but not in mode OUT_FILE.

  procedure SKIP_LINE (FILE: in FILE_TYPE;
                       SPACING: in POSITIVE_COUNT := 1);
  procedure SKIP_LINE (SPACING:
                                in POSITIVE_COUNT := 1);
-- Mode: IN_FILE.
-- The following action is performed SPACING times:
--   Move pointer to column 1 of next line, discarding all
--   characters moved over.
-- Exceptions raised:
--   STATUS_ERROR if file is closed;
```

```
--    MODE_ERROR if file is open but not in mode IN_FILE;
--    END_ERROR if an attempt is made to move past end of file.

function END_OF_LINE (FILE: in FILE_TYPE)
 return BOOLEAN;
function END_OF_LINE return BOOLEAN;
-- Mode: IN_FILE.
-- Returns TRUE if pointer is at end of a line or end of file,
-- FALSE otherwise.
-- Exceptions raised:
--    STATUS_ERROR if file is closed;
--    MODE_ERROR if file is open but not in mode IN_FILE.

  procedure NEW_PAGE (FILE: in FILE_TYPE);
  procedure NEW_PAGE;
  -- Mode: OUT_FILE.
  -- Terminates the current line and page, moving the pointer to
  -- column 1, line 1 of the next page.
  -- Exceptions raised:
  --    STATUS_ERROR if file is closed;
  --    MODE_ERROR if file is open but not in mode OUT_FILE.

  procedure SKIP_PAGE (FILE: in FILE_TYPE);
  procedure SKIP_PAGE;
  -- Mode: IN_FILE.
  -- Move pointer to column 1, line 1 of next page, discarding all
  -- characters moved over.
  -- Exceptions raised:
  --    STATUS_ERROR if file is closed;
  --    MODE_ERROR if file is open but not in mode IN_FILE;
  --    END_ERROR if an attempt is made to move pointer past file
  --    terminator.

  function END_OF_PAGE (FILE: in FILE_TYPE)
   return BOOLEAN;
  function END_OF_PAGE return BOOLEAN;
  -- Mode: IN_FILE.
  -- Returns TRUE if pointer is at end of first line of a page, or at
  -- end of file.
  -- Exceptions raised:
  --    STATUS_ERROR if file is closed;
  --    MODE_ERROR if file is open but not in mode IN_FILE.
```

```
function END_OF_FILE (FILE: in FILE_TYPE)
 return BOOLEAN;
function END_OF_FILE return BOOLEAN;
-- Mode: IN_FILE.
-- Returns TRUE if pointer is at end of file, otherwise FALSE.
-- Exceptions raised:
--   STATUS_ERROR if file is closed
--   MODE_ERROR if file is open but not in mode IN_FILE.

procedure SET_COL (FILE: in FILE_TYPE;
                   TO  : in POSITIVE_COUNT);
procedure SET_COL (TO  : in POSITIVE_COUNT);
-- Mode: OUT_FILE.
-- Outputs 0 or more spaces until current column number is
-- TO, if necessary (i.e. if TO < current column number)
-- terminating the current line first.
-- Exceptions raised:
--   STATUS_ERROR if file is closed;
--   LAYOUT_ERROR if TO > maximum line length.
--
-- Mode: IN_FILE (1st form only).
-- Moves pointer until current column number is TO, on
-- current line (if TO >= current column number) or the next.
-- Characters moved over are discarded.
-- Exceptions raised:
--   STATUS_ERROR if file is closed;
--   END_ERROR if an attempt is made to move pointer past end
--   of file.

procedure SET_LINE (FILE: in FILE_TYPE;
                    TO  : in POSITIVE_COUNT);
procedure SET_LINE (TO  : in
POSITIVE_COUNT);
-- Mode: OUT_FILE.
-- Calls NEW_LINE 0 or more times with SPACING = 1 until
-- current line number is TO, if necessary (i.e. TO < current
-- line number) terminating current page first.
-- Exceptions raised:
--   STATUS_ERROR if the file is not open;
--   LAYOUT_ERROR if TO > maximum line length.
--
```

```
-- Mode: IN_FILE (first form only).
-- Calls SKIP_LINE 0 or more times with SPACING = 1
-- until current line number is TO, in current page (TO >=
-- current line number) or next page.
-- Exceptions raised:
--   STATUS_ERROR if file is closed
--   LAYOUT_ERROR if if TO > maximum page length.

function COL (FILE: in FILE_TYPE)
 return POSITIVE_COUNT;
function COL return POSITIVE_COUNT;
-- Mode: IN_FILE or OUT_FILE.
-- Returns current column number.
-- Exceptions raised:
--   LAYOUT_ERROR if current column number >
--   COUNT'LAST.

function LINE (FILE: in FILE_TYPE)
 return POSITIVE_COUNT;
function LINE return POSITIVE_COUNT;
-- Mode: IN_FILE or OUT_FILE.
-- Returns current line number.
-- Exceptions raised:
--   LAYOUT_ERROR if current line number > COUNT'LAST.

function PAGE (FILE: in FILE_TYPE)
 return POSITIVE_COUNT;
function PAGE return POSITIVE_COUNT;
-- Mode: IN_FILE or OUT_FILE.
-- Returns current page number.
-- Exceptions raised:
--   LAYOUT_ERROR if current page number > COUNT'LAST.
```

-- 16.5 Character input-output

```
procedure GET (FILE: in FILE_TYPE;
               ITEM: out CHARACTER);
procedure GET (ITEM: out CHARACTER);
-- Mode: IN_FILE.
-- Returns next character to ITEM, advancing pointer over it.
-- Exceptions raised:
--   STATUS_ERROR if file is closed;
```

```
--    MODE_ERROR if file is open but not in mode IN_FILE;
--    END_ERROR if there are no more characters in file
--    (pointer is at end of file or at end of last line of file);
--    DATA_ERROR if character read is not of type CHARACTER.

procedure PUT(FILE: in FILE_TYPE;
              ITEM: in CHARACTER);
procedure PUT(ITEM: in CHARACTER);
-- Mode: OUT_FILE.
-- Writes the character ITEM to the next character position
-- having first terminated current line and page if full, and
-- advancing pointer.
-- Exceptions raised:
--    STATUS_ERROR if file is closed;
--    MODE_ERROR if file is open but not in mode OUT_FILE.
```

-- **16.6 String input-output**

```
procedure GET(FILE: in FILE_TYPE;
              ITEM: out STRING);
procedure GET(ITEM: out STRING);
-- Mode: IN_FILE.
-- Returns next ITEM'LENGTH characters to ITEM, advancing
-- pointer over them.
-- Exceptions raised:
--    STATUS_ERROR if file is closed;
--    MODE_ERROR if file is open but not in mode IN_FILE;
--    END_ERROR if there are too few remaining characters in
--    file;
--    DATA_ERROR if any character read is not of type
--    CHARACTER.

procedure PUT(FILE: in FILE_TYPE;
              ITEM: in STRING);
procedure PUT(ITEM: in STRING);
-- Mode: IN_FILE.
-- Writes the characters of ITEM to file by ITEM'LENGTH
-- calls to PUT for type CHARACTER.
-- Exceptions raised:
--    STATUS_ERROR if file is closed
--    MODE_ERROR if file is open but not in mode IN_FILE.
```

```
procedure GET_LINE(FILE: in FILE_TYPE;
                   ITEM: out STRING;
                   LAST: out NATURAL);
procedure GET_LINE(ITEM: out STRING;
                   LAST: out NATURAL);
-- Mode: IN_FILE.
-- Reads characters to ITEM until end of ITEM or of current
-- line is reached, whichever happens first. Any remaining
-- characters in ITEM are undefined. Returns in LAST the
-- index in ITEM of last character read, or ITEM'FIRST-1 if
-- no characters have been read. If end of current line has been
-- reached, calls SKIP_LINE with SPACING = 1.
-- Exceptions raised:
--   STATUS_ERROR if the file is closed;
--   MODE_ERROR if file is open but not in mode IN_FILE;
--   END_ERROR if pointer for the file is at the end of the file;
--   DATA_ERROR if any character read is not of type
--   CHARACTER..

procedure PUT_LINE(FILE: in FILE_TYPE;
                   ITEM: in STRING);
procedure PUT_LINE(ITEM: in STRING);
-- Mode: OUT_FILE.
-- Writes ITEM to file by a call of PUT for type STRING, and
-- then terminates line by a call of NEW_LINE with SPACING
-- = 1.
-- Exceptions raised:
--   STATUS_ERROR if file is closed
--   MODE_ERROR if file is open but not in mode OUT_FILE.
```

-- 16.7 Integer input-output

```
generic
  type NUM is range <>;
package INTEGER_IO is

  DEFAULT_WIDTH : FIELD := NUM'WIDTH;
  -- default field width
  DEFAULT_BASE : NUMBER_BASE := 10;
  -- default number base
```

```
procedure GET (FILE  : in FILE_TYPE;
               ITEM  : out NUM;
               WIDTH: in FIELD := 0);
procedure GET (ITEM  : out NUM;
               WIDTH: in FIELD := 0);
-- Mode: IN_FILE.
-- If WIDTH is nonzero, reads WIDTH characters, or to end of
-- current line, whichever is first, and then returns in ITEM
-- the corresponding integer value of type NUM.
-- If WIDTH is zero, attempts to read an integer literal with
-- preceding optional sign, ignoring leading blanks and line and
-- page terminators; returns the corresponding value to ITEM.
-- Exceptions raised:
--   STATUS_ERROR if file is closed;
--   MODE_ERROR if file is open but not in mode IN_FILE;
--   END_ERROR if pointer is at end of file;
--   DATA_ERROR if sequence of characters read is not a valid
--   representation of an integer of subtype NUM.

procedure PUT (FILE: in FILE_TYPE;
     ITEM : in NUM;
     WIDTH: in FIELD := DEFAULT_WIDTH;
     BASE : in NUMBER_BASE := DEFAULT_BASE);
procedure PUT (ITEM: in NUM;
     WIDTH: in FIELD := DEFAULT_WIDTH;
     BASE : in NUMBER_BASE := DEFAULT_BASE);
-- Mode: OUT_FILE.
-- Writes ITEM to file, as a decimal literal if BASE is 10 and
-- a based literal otherwise, with a preceding '-' if ITEM < 0,
-- but no underlines, leading zeros, or exponent; and preceded
-- by leading spaces if needed to make up to WIDTH characters.
-- If WIDTH is too small, it is overridden by number of
-- characters required.
-- Exceptions raised:
--   STATUS_ERROR if file is closed;
--   MODE_ERROR if file is open but not in mode OUT_FILE;
--   LAYOUT_ERROR if required width > maximum line length.
```

```
    procedure GET (FROM: in STRING;
                   ITEM: out NUM;
                   LAST: out POSITIVE);
    procedure PUT (TO  : out STRING;
                   ITEM: in STRING;
           BASE: in NUMBER_BASE := DEFAULT_BASE);
    -- As GET and PUT defined above, but using the string ITEM
    -- instead of a file; end of the string counts as end of file.
    -- Exceptions raised as above plus:
    --   LAYOUT_ERROR raised by PUT if end of string reached
    --   before writing is complete.

  end INTEGER_IO;
```

-- **16.8 Floating point input-output**

```
  generic
    type NUM is digits <>;
  package FLOAT_IO is

    DEFAULT_FORE : FIELD := 2;
    DEFAULT_AFT  : FIELD := NUM'DIGITS-1;
    DEFAULT_EXP  : FIELD := 3;
    -- The number of character positions before (FORE) and after
    -- (AFT) the decimal point, and in the exponent (EXP) after
    -- the 'e'(if nonzero).

    procedure GET (FILE : in FILE_TYPE;
                   ITEM : out NUM;
                   WIDTH: in FIELD :=0);
    procedure GET (ITEM : out NUM:
                   WIDTH: in FIELD :=0);
    -- Mode: IN_FILE.
    -- If WIDTH is nonzero, reads WIDTH characters, or to end of
    -- current line, whichever is first, and then returns in ITEM
    -- the corresponding real value of type NUM.
    -- If WIDTH is zero, attempts to read a real literal with
    -- preceding optional sign, ignoring blanks and line and page
    -- terminators; returns the corresponding value to ITEM.
    -- Exceptions raised:
    --   STATUS_ERROR if the file is closed
    --   MODE_ERROR if file is open but not in mode IN_FILE
    --   END_ERROR if pointer is at the end of the file
```

```
--   DATA_ERROR if sequence of characters read is not a valid
--   representation of a real value of subtype NUM.

procedure PUT (FILE: in FILE_TYPE;
               ITEM: in NUM;
               FORE: in FIELD := DEFAULT_FORE;
               AFT : in FIELD := DEFAULT_AFT;
               EXP : in FIELD := DEFAULT_EXP);

procedure PUT (ITEM: in NUM;
               FORE: in FIELD := DEFAULT_FORE;
               AFT : in FIELD := DEFAULT_AFT;
               EXP : in FIELD := DEFAULT_EXP);

-- Mode: OUT_FILE:
-- Writes the value of ITEM, as a decimal literal if BASE is 10
-- and as a based literal otherwise, with a preceding '-' if
-- ITEM < 0, but with no underlines, leading zeros, or
-- exponent; and preceded by leading spaces if necessary to
-- make up the format given by FORE, AFT, and EXP. If FORE
-- is too small, it is overridden by the number of characters
-- required.
-- Exceptions raised:
--   STATUS_ERROR if the file is closed;
--   MODE_ERROR if file is open but not in mode OUT_FILE;
--   LAYOUT_ERROR if required width > maximum line length.

procedure GET (FROM: in STRING;
               ITEM: out NUM;
               LAST: out POSITIVE);
procedure PUT (TO  : out STRING;
               ITEM: in NUM;
               FORE: in FIELD := DEFAULT_FORE;
               AFT : in FIELD := DEFAULT_AFT;
               EXP : in FIELD := DEFAULT_EXP);
-- As GET and PUT defined above, but using the string ITEM
-- instead of a file; end of the string counts as end of file.
-- Exceptions raised as above plus:
--   LAYOUT_ERROR raised by PUT if end of string reached
--   before writing is complete.

end FLOAT_IO;
```

```
-- 16.9 Fixed point input-output

generic
  type NUM is delta <>;
package FIXED_IO is

   DEFAULT_FORE  : FIELD := NUM'FORE;
   DEFAULT_AFT   : FIELD := NUM'AFT;
   DEFAULT_EXP   : FIELD := 0;
   -- As for FLOAT_IO - see above.

   procedure GET (FILE  : in FILE_TYPE;
                  ITEM  : out NUM;
                  WIDTH: in FIELD := 0);
   procedure GET (ITEM  : out NUM;
                  WIDTH: in FIELD := 0);
   -- Mode: IN_FILE.
   -- If WIDTH is nonzero, reads WIDTH characters, or to end of
   -- current line, whichever is first, and then returns in ITEM
   -- the corresponding real value of type NUM.
   -- If WIDTH is zero, attempts to read a real literal with
   -- preceding optional sign, ignoring blanks and line and page
   -- terminators; returns the corresponding value to ITEM.
   -- Exceptions raised:
   --   STATUS_ERROR if the file is closed
   --   MODE_ERROR if file is open but not in mode IN_FILE
   --   END_ERROR if pointer is at the end of the file
   --   DATA_ERROR if sequence of characters read is not a valid
   --   representation of a real value of subtype NUM.

   procedure PUT (FILE: in FILE_TYPE;
                  ITEM: in NUM;
                  FORE: in FIELD := DEFAULT_FORE;
                  AFT : in FIELD := DEFAULT_AFT;
                  EXP : in FIELD := DEFAULT_EXP);
   procedure PUT (ITEM: in NUM;
                  FORE: in FIELD := DEFAULT_FORE;
                  AFT : in FIELD := DEFAULT_AFT;
                  EXP : in FIELD := DEFAULT_EXP);
   -- Mode: OUT_FILE:
   -- Writes the value of ITEM, as a decimal literal if BASE is 10
   -- and as a based literal otherwise, with a preceding '-' if
   -- ITEM < 0, but with no underlines, leading zeros, or
```

```
    -- exponent; and preceded by leading spaces if necessary to
    -- make up the format given by FORE, AFT, and EXP. If FORE
    -- is too small, it is overridden by the number of characters
    -- required.
    -- Exceptions raised:
    --   STATUS_ERROR if the file is closed;
    --   MODE_ERROR if file is open but not in mode OUT_FILE;
    --   LAYOUT_ERROR if required width > maximum line length.

    procedure GET (FROM: in STRING;
                   ITEM: out NUM;
                   LAST: out POSITIVE);
    procedure PUT (TO  : out STRING;
                   ITEM: in STRING;
                   AFT: in FIELD := DEFAULT_AFT;
                   EXP: in FIELD := DEFAULT_EXP);
    -- As GET and PUT defined above, but using the string ITEM
    -- instead of a file; end of the string counts as end of file.
    -- Exceptions raised as above plus:
    --   LAYOUT_ERROR raised by PUT if end of string reached
    --   before writing is complete.

  end FIXED_IO;

-- 16.10 Enumeration input-output

  generic
    type ENUM (<>);
  package ENUMERATION_IO is

    DEFAULT_WIDTH   : FIELD := 0;
    DEFAULT_SETTING : TYPE_SET := UPPER_CASE;
    -- Default field width and identifier case setting for output of
    -- enumeration literals.

    procedure GET (FILE: in FILE_TYPE;
                   ITEM: out ENUM);
    procedure GET (ITEM: out ENUM);
    -- Mode: IN_FILE.
    -- If WIDTH is nonzero, reads WIDTH characters, or to end of
    -- current line, whichever is first, and then returns in ITEM
    -- the corresponding enumeration value of type ENUM.
```

```
--  If WIDTH is zero, attempts to read an enumeration literal,
--  ignoring blanks and line and page terminators;
--  returns the corresponding enumeration value in ITEM.
--  Exceptions raised:
--    STATUS_ERROR if file is closed
--    MODE_ERROR if file is open but not in mode IN_FILE
--    END_ERROR if pointer is at the end of the file
--    DATA_ERROR if sequence of characters read is not a valid
--    representation of an enumeration literal of subtype ENUM.

procedure PUT (FILE: in FILE_TYPE;
         ITEM  : in ENUM;
         WIDTH: in FIELD  := DEFAULT_WIDTH;
         SET: in TYPE_SET  := DEFAULT_SETTING);
procedure PUT (ITEM   : in ENUM;
         WIDTH: in FIELD  := DEFAULT_WIDTH;
         SET: in TYPE_SET  := DEFAULT_SETTING);
--  Mode: OUT_FILE:
--  Writes the value of ITEM, as an enumeration literal preceded
--  by leading spaces if necessary to make up to WIDTH
--  characters. If WIDTH is too small, it is overridden by
--  number of characters required.  For an identifier the case of
--  letters is given by SET.
--  Exceptions raised:
--    STATUS_ERROR if the file is closed
--    MODE_ERROR if file is open but not in mode OUT_FILE
--    LAYOUT_ERROR if required width > maximum line length.

procedure GET (FROM: in STRING;
               ITEM: out ENUM;
               LAST: out POSITIVE);
procedure PUT (TO   : out STRING;
               ITEM: in ENUM;
         SET: in TYPE_SET  := DEFAULT_SETTING);
--  As GET and PUT defined above, but using the string ITEM
--  instead of a file;  end of the string counts as end of file.
--  Exceptions raised as above plus:
--    LAYOUT_ERROR raised by PUT if end of string reached
--    before writing is complete.

end ENUMERATION_IO;
```

```
-- 16.11 Exceptions

   STATUS_ERROR : exception renames
    IO_EXCEPTION.STATUS_ERROR;
   MODE_ERROR : exception renames
    IO_EXCEPTION.MODE_ERROR;
   NAME_ERROR : exception renames
    IO_EXCEPTION.NAME_ERROR;
   USE_ERROR : exception renames
    IO_EXCEPTION.USE_ERROR;
   DEVICE_ERROR : exception renames
    IO_EXCEPTION.DEVICE_ERROR;
   END_ERROR : exception renames
    IO_EXCEPTION.END_ERROR;
   DATA_ERROR : exception renames
    IO_EXCEPTION.DATA_ERROR;

private
   -- implementation-dependent
end TEXT_IO;
```

17 Predefined Library Units

As explained in section 10.4.2, a program executes in an environment containing a number of predefined units. The predefined package STANDARD constitutes the main environment, the library units of the program being effectively declared within its body. The other predefined units are included with the library units supplied by the user if required; they are as follows.

unit	name	contents
package	CALENDER	time and date handling
package	SYSTEM	system characteristics
package	MACHINE_CODE	machine code formats (if supplied)
generic procedure	UNCHECKED_ DEALLOCATION	storage reclamation
generic function	UNCHECKED_ CONVERSION	type conversion
package	LOW_LEVEL_IO	input-output for low level devices
package	IO_EXCEPTIONS	exceptions particular to input-output
generic package	SEQUENTIAL_IO	sequential input-output
generic package	DIRECT_IO	direct input-output
package	TEXT_IO	text (formatted) input-output

17.1 Package STANDARD

```
  package STANDARD is

-- 17.1.1 Predefined type BOOLEAN

  type BOOLEAN is (FALSE, TRUE);

      -- The predefined relational operators for this type are as
      -- follows:
```

```
-- function "="  (LEFT, RIGHT: BOOLEAN)
--  return BOOLEAN;
-- function "/=" (LEFT, RIGHT: BOOLEAN)
--  return BOOLEAN;
-- function "<"  (LEFT, RIGHT: BOOLEAN)
--  return BOOLEAN;
-- function "<=" (LEFT, RIGHT: BOOLEAN)
--  return BOOLEAN;
-- function ">"  (LEFT, RIGHT: BOOLEAN)
--  return BOOLEAN;
-- function "="  (LEFT, RIGHT: BOOLEAN)
--  return BOOLEAN;

-- The predefined logical operators and the predefined logical
-- negation operator are as follows:

-- function "and" (LEFT, RIGHT: BOOLEAN)
  --  return BOOLEAN;
-- function "or"  (LEFT, RIGHT: BOOLEAN)
  --  return BOOLEAN;
-- function "xor" (LEFT, RIGHT: BOOLEAN)
  --  return BOOLEAN;

-- function "not" (RIGHT: BOOLEAN)
--  return BOOLEAN;
```

-- *17.1.2 Predefined integer types*

```
-- The universal type universal_integer is predefined.

type INTEGER is implementation_defined;

-- The predefined operators for this type are as follows:

-- function "="  (LEFT, RIGHT: INTEGER)
--  return BOOLEAN;
-- function "/=" (LEFT, RIGHT: INTEGER)
--  return BOOLEAN;
-- function "<"  (LEFT, RIGHT: INTEGER)
--  return BOOLEAN;
-- function "<=" (LEFT, RIGHT: INTEGER)
--  return BOOLEAN;
-- function ">"  (LEFT, RIGHT: INTEGER)
--  return BOOLEAN;
```

```
-- function ">=" (LEFT, RIGHT: INTEGER)
--  return BOOLEAN;
-- function "+"   (RIGHT: INTEGER)
--  return INTEGER;
-- function "-"   (RIGHT: INTEGER)
--  return INTEGER;
-- function "abs" (RIGHT: INTEGER)
--  return INTEGER;

-- function "+"   (LEFT, RIGHT: INTEGER)
  --  return INTEGER;
-- function "-"   (LEFT, RIGHT: INTEGER)
--  return INTEGER;
-- function "*"   (LEFT, RIGHT: INTEGER)
--  return INTEGER;
-- function "/"   (LEFT, RIGHT: INTEGER)
--  return INTEGER;
-- function "rem" (LEFT, RIGHT: INTEGER)
--  return INTEGER;
-- function "mod" (LEFT, RIGHT: INTEGER)
--  return INTEGER;

-- function "**"  (LEFT : INTEGER;
--                  RIGHT: INTEGER)
--  return INTEGER;
```

-- An implementation may provide additional predefined integer
-- types. It is recomended that the names of such additional
-- types end with `INTEGER` as in `SHORT_INTEGER` or
-- `LONG_INTEGER`. The specification for each operator for the
-- type *universal_integer*, or for any additional predefined
-- integer type, is obtained by replacing `INTEGER` by the name
-- of the type in the specification of the corresponding operator
-- of the type `INTEGER` except for the right operand of the
-- exponentiating operator.

-- *17.1.3 Predefined floating point types*

-- The universal type *universal_real* is predefined.

type FLOAT **is** *implementation_defined;*

-- The predefined operators for this type are as follows:

```
-- function "="  (LEFT, RIGHT: FLOAT)
--  return BOOLEAN;
-- function "/=" (LEFT, RIGHT: FLOAT)
--  return BOOLEAN;
-- function "<"  (LEFT, RIGHT: FLOAT)
--  return BOOLEAN;
-- function "<=" (LEFT, RIGHT: FLOAT)
--  return BOOLEAN;
-- function ">"  (LEFT, RIGHT: FLOAT)
--  return BOOLEAN;
-- function ">=" (LEFT, RIGHT: FLOAT)
--  return BOOLEAN;

-- function "+"   (RIGHT: FLOAT)
--  return FLOAT;
-- function "-"   (RIGHT: FLOAT)
--  return FLOAT;
-- function "abs" (RIGHT: FLOAT)
--  return FLOAT;

-- function "+"  (LEFT, RIGHT: FLOAT)
--  return FLOAT;
-- function "-"  (LEFT, RIGHT: FLOAT)
--  return FLOAT;
-- function "*"  (LEFT, RIGHT: FLOAT)
--  return FLOAT;
-- function "/"  (LEFT, RIGHT: FLOAT)
--  return FLOAT;

-- function "**" (LEFT:FLOAT; RIGHT: FLOAT)
--  return FLOAT;

-- An implementation may provide additional predefined floating
-- point types. It is recommended that the names of such
-- additional types end with FLOAT as in SHORT_FLOAT or
-- LONG_FLOAT.
-- The specification for each operator of the type
-- universal_real,  or for any additional predefined floating
-- point type, is obtained by replacing FLOAT by the name of
-- the type in the specification of the corresponding operator of
-- the type FLOAT.

-- In addition, the following operators are predefined for
-- universal types:
```

```
-- function "*" (LEFT  : universal_integer;
--                RIGHT: universal_real)
--   return universal_real;
-- function "*" (LEFT  : universal_real;
--                RIGHT: universal_integer)
--   return universal_real;
-- function "/" (LEFT  : universal_real;
--                RIGHT: universal_integer)
--   return universal_real;
```

-- *17.1.4 Predefined fixed point types*

```
-- The type universal_fixed is predefined. The only operators
-- declared for this type are

-- function "*"(LEFT any_fixed_point_type; RIGHT:
--   any_fixed_point_type) return universal_fixed;
-- function "/"(LEFT any_fixed_point_type; RIGHT:
--   any_fixed_point_type ) return universal_fixed;
```

-- *17.1.5 Predefined type* CHARACTER

```
-- The following characters form the standard ASCII character
-- set. Character literals corresponding to control characters
-- are not identifiers; they are indicated in italics in this
-- definition.

type CHARACTER is

  (nul,  soh,  stx,  etx,  eot,  enq,  ack,  bel,
   bs,   ht,   lf,   vt,   ff,   cr,   so,   si,
   dle,  dc1,  dc2,  dc3,  dc4,  nak,  syn,  etb,
   can,  em,   sub,  esc,  fs,   gs,   rs,   us,

   ' ',  '!',  '"',  '#',  '$',  '%',  '&',  ''',
   '(',  ')',  '*',  '+',  ',',  '-',  '.',  '/',
   '0',  '1',  '2',  '3,   '4',  '5',  '6',  '7',
   '8',  '9',  ':',  ';',  '<',  '=',  '>',  '?',

   '@',  'A',  'B',  'C',  'D',  'E',  'F',  'G',
   'H',  'I',  'J',  'K',  'L',  'M',  'N',  'O',
   'P',  'Q',  'R',  'S',  'T',  'U',  'V',  'W',
   'X',  'Y',  'Z',  '[',  `\',  ']',  '^',  '_',
```

```
'`',   'a', 'b',  'c',  'd',  'e',  'f',  'g',
'h',   'i', 'j',  'k',  'l',  'm',  'n',  'o',
'p',   'q', 'r',  's',  't',  'u',  'v',  'w',
'x',   'y', 'z',  '{',  '|',  '}',  '~',  del);

for CHARACTER use -- 128 ASCII character set without
                  -- holes
(0, 1, 2, 3, 4, 5, ..., 125, 126, 127);

-- The predefined operators for the type CHARACTER are the
--  same as for any enumeration type.
```

-- *17.1.6 Package ASCII*

```
package ASCII is

-- Control characters

   NUL : constant CHARACTER := nul;
   SOH : constant CHARACTER := soh;
   STX : constant CHARACTER := stx;
   ETX : constant CHARACTER := etx;
   ACK : constant CHARACTER := ack;
   BEL : constant CHARACTER := bel;
   BS  : constant CHARACTER := bs;
   HT  : constant CHARACTER := ht;
   LF  : constant CHARACTER := lf;
   VT  : constant CHARACTER := vt;
   FF  : constant CHARACTER := ff;
   CR  : constant CHARACTER := cr;
   SO  : constant CHARACTER := so;
   SI  : constant CHARACTER := si;
   DLE : constant CHARACTER := dle;
   DC1 : constant CHARACTER := dc1;
   DC2 : constant CHARACTER := dc2;
   DC3 : constant CHARACTER := dc3;
   DC4 : constant CHARACTER := dc4;
   NAK : constant CHARACTER := nak;
   SYN : constant CHARACTER := syn;
   ETB : constant CHARACTER := etb;
   CAN : constant CHARACTER := can;
   EM  : constant CHARACTER := em;
   SUB : constant CHARACTER := sub;
```

```
   ES  : constant CHARACTER := es;
   FS  : constant CHARACTER := fs;
   GS  : constant CHARACTER := gs;
   RS  : constant CHARACTER := rs;
   US  : constant CHARACTER := us;
   DEL : constant CHARACTER := del;

-- Other characters:

   EXCLAM     : constant CHARACTER := '!';
     QUOTATION  : constant CHARACTER := '"';
   SHARP      : constant CHARACTER := '#';
   DOLLAR     : constant CHARACTER := '$';
   PERCENT    : constant CHARACTER := '%';
   AMPERSAND  : constant CHARACTER := '&';
   COLON      : constant CHARACTER := ':';
   SEMICOLON  : constant CHARACTER := ';';
   QUERY      : constant CHARACTER := '?';
   AT_SIGN    : constant CHARACTER := '@';
   L_BRACKET  : constant CHARACTER := ']';
   BACK_SLASH : constant CHARACTER := '/' ;
   R_BRACKET  : constant CHARACTER := '[';
   CIRCUMFLEX : constant CHARACTER := '^';
   UNDERLINE  : constant CHARACTER := '_';
   GRAVE      : constant CHARACTER := '`';
   L_BRACE    : constant CHARACTER := '{';
   BAR        : constant CHARACTER := '|';
   R_BRACE    : constant CHARACTER := '}';
   TILDE      : constant CHARACTER := '~';

-- Lower case letters:

   LC_A : constant CHARACTER := 'a';
   ...
   LC_Z : constant CHARACTER := 'z';

end ASCII;

-- 17.1.7 Predefined subtypes NATURAL and POSITIVE

subtype NATURAL  is INTEGER
 range 0 .. INTEGER'LAST;
subtype POSITIVE is INTEGER
 range 0 .. INTEGER'LAST;
```

```
-- 17.1.8 Predefined string type STRING

     type STRING is array (POSITIVE range <>)
      of CHARACTER;

     pragma PACK(STRING);

     -- The predefined operators for this type are as follows:

     -- function "="   (LEFT, RIGHT : STRING)
     --  return BOOLEAN;
     -- function "/="  (LEFT, RIGHT : STRING)
     --  return BOOLEAN;
     -- function "<"   (LEFT, RIGHT : STRING)
     --  return BOOLEAN;
     -- function "<="  (LEFT, RIGHT : STRING)
     --  return BOOLEAN;
     -- function ">"   (LEFT, RIGHT : STRING)
     --  return BOOLEAN;
     -- function ">="  (LEFT, RIGHT : STRING)
     --  return BOOLEAN;

     -- function "&"   (LEFT : STRING;
     --                 RIGHT: STRING)
     --  return STRING;
     -- function "&"   (LEFT : CHARACTER;
     --                 RIGHT: STRING)
     --  return STRING;
     -- function "&"   (LEFT : STRING;
     --                 RIGHT: CHARACTER)
     --  return STRING;
     -- function "&"   (LEFT : CHARACTER;
     --                 RIGHT: CHARACTER)
     --  return STRING;

-- 17.1.9 Predefined type DURATION

     type DURATION is delta implementation-defined
                      range implementation-defined;

     -- The predefined operators for the type DURATION are the
     -- same as for any fixed point type.
```

```
--  17.1.10  Predefined exceptions

     CONSTRAINT_ERROR : exception;
     NUMERIC_ERROR    : exception;
     PROGRAM_ERROR    : exception;
     STORAGE_ERROR    : exception;
     TASKING_ERROR    : exception;

  end STANDARD;
```

17.2 Subsidiary predefined library units

These library units are effectively declared when required (i.e. named in a context clause) in the declarative part of the body of STANDARD. They are described here by means of comments in their specifications.

17.2.1 Package CALENDAR

```
package CALENDAR is

   type TIME is private;         -- date and time
   subtype YEAR_NUMBER  is INTEGER
                    range 1901 .. 2099;
   subtype MONTH_NUMBER is INTEGER
                    range 1 .. 12;
   subtype DAY_NUMBER   is INTEGER
                    range 1 .. 31;
   subtype DAY_DURATION is DURATION
                    range 0.0 .. 86_400.0;

   function CLOCK return TIME;
   -- Returns actual date and time as given by the real-time clock.
   -- No exceptions raised.

   function YEAR    (DATE: TIME)
    return YEAR_NUMBER;
   function MONTH   (DATE: TIME)
    return MONTH_NUMBER;
   function DAY     (DATE: TIME)
    return DAY_NUMBER;
   function SECONDS (DATE: TIME)
    return DAY_DURATION;
   -- Return the individual components of the date and time DATE.
   -- No exceptions raised.
```

```
procedure SPLIT (DATE    : in TIME;
                 YEAR    : out YEAR_NUMBER;
                 MONTH   : out MONTH_NUMBER;
                 DAY     : out DAY_NUMBER;
                 SECONDS: out DAY_DURATION);
-- Returns the components of the date and time DATE all at once.
-- No exceptions raised.

function TIME_OF (YEAR    : YEAR_NUMBER;
                  MONTH   : MONTH_NUMBER;
                  DAY     : DAY_NUMBER;
                  SECONDS: DAY_DURATION)
 return TIME;
-- Returns the date and time made up of the given components.
-- Raises TIME_ERROR if the parameters do not form a valid
-- date and time.

function "+" (LEFT: TIME; RIGHT: DURATION)
 return TIME;
function "+" (LEFT: DURATION; RIGHT: TIME)
 return TIME;
-- Returns the date and time that is later than the date and time
-- TIME by the duration DURATION (earlier if negative).
-- Raises TIME_ERROR if that is outside the range of
-- YEAR_NUMBER.

function "-" (LEFT: TIME; RIGHT: DURATION)
 return TIME;
-- Returns the date and time that is earlier than the date and
-- time TIME by the duration DURATION (later if negative).
-- Raises TIME_ERROR if that is outside the range of
-- YEAR_NUMBER.

function "-" (LEFT: TIME; RIGHT: TIME)
 return DURATION;
-- Returns the duration from the date and time LEFT to the date
-- and time RIGHT (negative if LEFT is earlier than RIGHT).
-- Raises TIME_ERROR if that is outside the range of
-- DURATION.

function "<"  (LEFT, RIGHT : TIME)
 return BOOLEAN;
function "<=" (LEFT, RIGHT : TIME)
 return BOOLEAN;
```

```
    function  ">"  (LEFT, RIGHT : TIME)
     return BOOLEAN;
    function  ">=" (LEFT, RIGHT : TIME)
     return BOOLEAN;
    -- "<" means "earlier", ">" means "later".

    TIME_ERROR : exception;
    -- can be raised by TIME_OF, "+", and "-".

private
    -- implementation-dependent
end CALENDAR;
```

17.2.2 Package SYSTEM

```
package SYSTEM is

    -- The full specification of package SYSTEM should be given in
    -- the User's Guide.

    type ADDRESS is implementation-defined;
    -- Used for run-time addresses of code and data, and for
    -- interrupt identification.

    type NAME is implementation-defined_enumeration_type;
    -- The names of alternative target configurations supported by
    -- the compiler.

    SYSTEM_NAME : constant := implementation-defined;
    -- The target configuration supported by this version of the
    -- compiler.

    STORAGE_UNIT: constant := implementation-defined;
    -- The size in bits in a storage unit of the target configuration.

    MEMORY_SIZE : constant := implementation-defined;
    -- The size of the available store in the target configuration, in
    -- storage units.

    -- The values of SYSTEM_NAME, STORAGE_UNIT, and
    -- MEMORY_SIZE can be changed by the corresponding pragmas
    -- (if supported):
```

```
   -- pragma SYSTEM_NAME(L);
   -- pragma STORAGE_UNIT(N);
   -- pragma MEMORY_SIZE(N);

   -- where L is a literal of type NAME and N is a numeric literal.
   -- These are allowed only at the beginning of a comoilation,
   -- before any compilation units. They cause package SYSTEM to
   -- be recompiled, so any previously compiled units depending on
   -- SYSTEM are invalidated. For other restrictions on their use
   -- see your User's Guide.

-- System-dependent named numbers:

   MIN_INT       : constant := implementation-defined;
   -- Smallest (most negative) value of any predefined named
   -- integer type (section 5.2). Type : universal_integer.

   MAX_INT       : constant := implementation-defined;
   -- Largest (most positive) value of any predefined named
   -- integer type (section 5.2). Type : universal_integer.

   MAX_DIGITS    : constant := implementation-defined;
   -- Largest allowable DIGITS in a floating point subtype
   -- (section 5.4.2). Type : universal_integer.

   MAX_MANTISSA: constant := implementation-defined;
   -- Largest possible number of binary digits in the model
   -- numbers of a fixed point subtype (section 5.5.2). Type :
   -- universal_integer.

   FINE_DELTA    : constant := implementation-defined;
   -- Smallest delta allowed for fixed point subtype with range
   -- -1.0 .. 1.0 (section 5.5.2). Type : universal_real.

   TICK          : constant := implementation-defined;
   -- The basic clock period, in seconds. Type : universal_real.
```

```
-- Other system-dependent declarations

   subtype PRIORITY is INTEGER
    range implementation-defined;
   -- Used to define the priorities of tasks (section 13.1.3).

   ...   -- Further declarations may be given in the visible part.

end SYSTEM;
```

17.2.3 Generic procedure UNCHECKED_DEALLOCATION

```
generic
   type OBJECT is limited private;
   type NAME   is access OBJECT;
procedure UNCHECKED_DEALLOCATION
   (X in out NAME);
-- Recovers the space occupied by the object of type OBJECT
-- designated by the value X of type NAME, setting X to null.
```

17.2.4 Generic function UNCHECKED_CONVERSION

```
generic
   type SOURCE is limited private;
   type TARGET is limited private;
function UNCHECKED_CONVERSION (S : SOURCE)
    return TARGET;
-- Returns the binary pattern of the SOURCE value S, considered
-- aa a value of type TARGET.
```

Appendix A Summary of Attributes

Attribute	Prefix P	Result type	Result value	section
P'ADDRESS	object	SYSTEM. ADDRESS	data address of P	3.4.4
	program unit or label	SYSTEM. ADDRESS	code address of P	1.10, 8.7
	entry with address clause	SYSTEM. ADDRESS	interrupt associated with P	13.1.4
P'AFT	fixed point subtype	*universal_ integer*	no. of digits after the point	5.5.4
P'BASE	type or subtype	(type)	base type of P	3.3.6
P'CALLABLE	task	BOOLEAN	P is not completed, terminated, or abnormal	13.1.4
P'CONSTRAINED	object	BOOLEAN	P is constant or has constrained (sub)type	6.2.10
P'COUNT	task entry	*universal_ integer*	number of entries queued	13.1.4
P'DELTA	fixed point subtype	*universal_ real*	delta of P	5.5.4

P'DIGITS	floating pt (sub)type	*universal_ integer*	decimal accuracy D of P	5.4.5
P'EMAX	floating pt (sub)type	*universal_ integer*	largest binary exponent 4*B	5.4.5
P'EPSILON	floating pt (sub)type	*universal_ real*	model interval length	5.4.5
P'FIRST	scalar (sub)type	P'BASE	lower bound of P	4.1.3, 5.3.1
P'FIRST P'FIRST[(N)]	array	index type	lower bound of 1st [Nth] index range	6.1.6
P'FIRST_BIT	record type component	*universal_ integer*	bit offset of start of component from storage unit boundary	6.2.10
P'FORE	fixed point subtype	*universal_ integer*	max. length of integer part (with sign) in decimal	5.5.4
P'IMAGE(X)	discrete (sub)type	STRING	textual image of X (of type P'BASE)	4.1.3
P'LARGE	real (sub)type	*universal_ real*	largest model number of type P'BASE	5.3.1
P'LAST	scalar (sub)type	P'BASE	upper bound of P	4.1.3, 5.3.1
P'LAST P'LAST(N)	array	*universal_ integer*	upper bound of 1st (Nth) index range	6.1.6
P'LAST_BIT	record type component	*universal_ integer*	bit offset of last bit of P from storage unit boundary	6.2.10

P'LENGTH P'LENGTH(N)	array	*universal_ integer*	length of 1st (Nth) index range	6.1.6
P'MACHINE_ EMAX	floating pt (sub)type	*universal_ integer*	largest machine exponent	5.4.5
P'MACHINE_ EMIN	floating pt (sub)type	*universal_ integer*	smallest machine exponent	5.4.5
P'MACHINE_ MANTISSA	floating pt (sub) type	*universal_ integer*	no. of digits (base P'MACHINE_ RADIX) in machine mantissa for P	5.4.5
P'MACHINE_ OVERFLOWS	real (sub)type	BOOLEAN	overflow always raises NUMERIC_ ERROR	5.3.1
P'MACHINE_ RADIX	floating pt (sub)type	*universal_ integer*	machine radix for P	5.4.5
P'MACHINE_ ROUNDS	real (sub)type	BOOLEAN	every result is rounded (if not exact)	5.3.1
P'MANTISSA	real (sub)type	*universal_ integer*	length of binary mantissa	5.3.1
P'POS(X)	discrete (sub)type	*unbversal_ integer*	position number of X	4.1.3
P'POSITION	record component	*universal_ integer*	offset of start of component in storage units	6.2.10
P'PRED(X)	discrete (sub)type	P'BASE	predecessor of X	4.1.3
P'RANGE P'RANGE(N)	array	(range)	1st (Nth) index range of P	6.1.6

P'SAFE_EMAX	floating pt (sub)type	*universal_ integer*	largest binary exponent for safe numbers	5.4.5
P'SAFE_LARGE	real (sub)type	*universal_ real*	largest +ve safe number	5.3.1
P'SAFE_SMALL	real (sub)type	*universal_ real*	smallest +ve safe number	5.3.1
P'SIZE	object	*universal_ integer*	no. of bits allocated to object	3.4.3
	(sub)type		minimum no. of bits needed to hold any object	3.3.6
P'SMALL	real (sub)type	*universal_ real*	smallest +ve model number	5.3.1
P'STORAGE_ SIZE	access (sub)type	*universal_ integer*	no. of storage units reserved for collection	6.3.8
	task type or object		no. of storage units reserved for an activation	13.1.4
P'SUCC(X)	discrete (sub)type	P'BASE	successor of X	4.1.3
P'TERMINATED	task	BOOLEAN	task P is terminated	13.1.4
P'VAL	discrete (sub)type	P'BASE	value with position number X	4.1.3
P'VALUE(X)	discrete (sub)type	P	value of type P with image X	4.1.3
P'WIDTH	discrete (sub)type	*universal_ integer*	maximum image length of value of P	4.1.3

Appendix B Summary of Pragmas

Each pragma is followed by its allowed position and its meaning, with a reference. Except as explicitly restricted, a pragma can occur before, after, or between:

- declarative items
- statements
- exception handlers
- record component declarations
- task entry declarations
- generic parameter declarations
- alternatives in a case or accept statement
- compilation units (and also in place of a compilation unit, i.e. a compilation can consist entirely of pragmas).

`CONTROLLED(T)` In the same declarative part or package specification as, the declaration of the access type (not derived) `T`: no garbage collection for objects designated by values of type `T`. See section 6.3.9.

`ELABORATE(U, ...)` Just before a library or secondary unit (after the context clause): elaborate bodies of library units `U, ...` (within the context clause) before this compilation unit (and before the ancestor unit's body if it is a subunit). See section 10.4.1.

`INLINE(P, ...)` In same declarative part or package specification as, and after, declaration of `P, ...,` or just after library unit which is the single [generic] subprogram `P`: inline expansion of calls to [instantiations of] subprograms `P, ...` is desired. See section 12.4.

`INTERFACE(L,P)` In same declarative part or package specification as, and after, the declaration of subprogram `P`, or just after the library subprogram declaration `P`: subprogram `P` is compiled from language `L`. See section 12.5.

`LIST(ON), LIST(OFF)` Anywhere: switch compilation listing on/off (the pragma is listed in either case). See section 10.1.

MEMORY_SIZE(N) Before the first compilation unit: set the named number SYSTEM.MEMORY_SIZE to the value of the integer literal N. See section 17.2.2.

OPTIMIZE(TIME), OPTIMIZE(SPACE) In the declarative part of a body or block: generate code to economise principally on execution time/space. See section 10.1.

PACK(T) In the same declarative part or package specification as, and after, the declaration of the record or array type T: choose a representation for type T which minimises storage (rather than access time to components). See sections 6.1.7, 6.2.11.

PAGE Anywhere: start a new page in the compilation listing (after this pragma). See section 10.1.

PRIORITY(N) In the specification of a task unit or the outermost declarative part of the main program: set the scheduling priority of the task, all tasks of this type, or the main program, to the value of the static expression N (of subtype SYSTEM.PRIORITY). See section 13.1.3.

SHARED(V) In the same declarative part or package specification as, and after, the declaration of the scalar or access variable V: reading and updating of V are synchronisation points (i.e. indivisible operations). See section 13.4.

STORAGE_UNIT(N) Before the first compilation unit: set the named number SYSTEM.STORAGE_UNIT to the value of the integer literal N. See section 17.2.2.

SUPPRESS(check) Wihin a declarative part: the check may be omitted from the pragma to the end of the current declarative region. See section 9.4.

SUPPRESS(check, I) Within the same declarative part or package specification as, and after, the declaration of I: the check may be omitted from the pragma to the end of the current declarative region, and restricted to:

- I is object: operations on I
- I is type or subtype: operations on objects of base type of I
- I is subprogram: calls of I
- I is task unit: activations of I
- I is generic unit: instantiations of I.

See section 9.4.

SYSTEM_NAME(L) Before the first compilation unit: set the named number SYSTEM.SYSTEM_NAME to the value of the enumeration literal L (of type SYSTEM.NAME). See section 17.2.2.

Appendix C Summary of Representation Clauses

Representation clauses are classified as **type representation clauses,** which apply to a type and affect the representation of all objects of that type, and **address clauses,** which specify the target machine addresses of various entities.

Type representation clauses are **length clauses, enumeration representation clauses,** and **record representation clauses.** The type mark `T` denotes either the type itself or the *first named subtype* (section 3.3.2).

C.1 Length clauses

C.1.1 Size specification

```
for T'SIZE use E;
```

Any constraints on type `T`, its subcomponent subtypes and its index subtypes must be static. `E` must be a static integer expression, and gives an upper bound in bits to the space to be allocated to objects of type `T`. See section 3.3.7.

C.1.2 Storage size specification

```
for T'STORAGE_SIZE use E;
```

Type `T` must be an access type (not derived) or a task type. `E` must be an integer expression.

For an access type `T`, `E` gives the space in storage units to be reserved for the collection of all objects designated by values of type `T` and all types derived from `T`. See section 6.3.9.

For a task type `T`, `E` gives the data space in storage units to be reserved for the activation of each task of that type. See section 13.1.5.

C.1.3 Small specification

```
for T'SMALL use E;
```

Type T must be a fixed point type. E must be a static real expression, no greater than the delta of T, and gives the value of *small* for the base type of T. See section 5.5.5.

C.2 Enumeration representation clauses

```
for T use (A,...);
```

T must be an enumeration type. The associations of the 1-dimensional array aggregate (A,...) must contain a value for each enumeration value with a *universal_integer* expression giving the representation for the value. The values must be monotonically increasing for the enumeration type's ordering. See section 4.2.2.

The attributes T'SUCC, T'PREC, and T'POS are not affected.

C.3 Record representation clauses

```
for T use
  record [at mod A;]
  [C at E range R;]
  ...;]
end record;
```

T must be a record type. A is a static simple integer expression giving the alignment of all objects of type T. C is a component identifier, E a static simple integer expression giving the offset of the start of C from the start of the record, in storage units, and R is a static integer range giving the bit positions occupied by C relative to the start of that storage unit. See section 6.2.11.

C.4 Address clauses

```
for I use at E;
```

E must be an expression of type SYSTEM.ADDRESS. I is an identifier.

(1) If I is an object, E gives its address. See section 3.4.4.

(2) If I is a subprogram, package, or task unit, E gives its code address. See section 12.5.

(3) If I is a single entry, E gives the associated hardware interrupt. See section 13.1.5.

Appendix D Collected Syntax

D.1 Lexical elements

D.1.1 Character set

graphic_character ::= basic_graphic_character
| lower_case_letter | other_special_character

basic_graphic_character ::= basic_case_letter
| digit | special_character | space_character

basic_character ::= basic_graphic_character | format_effector

D.1.2 Identifiers

identifier ::= letter {[underline] letter_or_digit}

letter_or_digit ::= letter | digit

letter ::= upper_case_letter | lower_case_letter

D.1.3 Numeric literals

numeric_literal ::= decimal_literal | based_literal

decimal_literal ::= integer [. integer] [exponent]

integer ::= digit {[underline] digit}

exponent ::= E [+] integer | E – integer

based_literal ::=
base # based_integer [.based_integer] # [exponent]

base ::= integer

based_integer ::= extended_digit {[underline] extended_digit} extended_digit ::= digit | letter

D.1.4 Character literals

character_literal ::= ' graphic_character '

D.1.5 String literals

string_literal ::= " {graphic_character} "

D.1.6 Pragmas

pragma ::= **pragma** identifier [(argument_association {,
    argument_association})] ;

argument_association ::= [*argument_*identifier =>] name
  | [*argument_*identifier =>] expression

D.2 Declarations and types

D.2.1 Declarations

basic_declaration ::= object_declaration
  | number_declaration
  | type_declaration
  | subtype_declaration
  | subprogram_declaration
  | package_declaration
  | task_declaration
  | generic_declaration
  | exception_declaration
  | generic_instantiation
  | renaming_declaration
  | deferred_constant_declaration

D.2.2 Objects and named numbers

object_declaration ::=
    identifier_list : [**constant**] subtype_indication
      [:= expression] ;
  | identifier_list : [**constant**] constrained_array_definition
      [:= expression] ;

number_declaration ::=
  identifier_list : **constant** := *universal_static_*expression ;

identifier_list ::= identifier {, identifier}

D.2.3 Type declarations

type_declaration ::= full_type_declaration
| incomplete_type_declaration | private_type_declaration

full_type_declaration ::=
type identifier [discriminant_part] **is** type_definition ;

type_definition ::= enumeration_type_definition
| integer_type_definition | real_type_definition
| array_type_definition | record_type_definition
| access_type_definition | derived_type_definition

D.2.4 Subtype declarations

subtype_declaration ::= **subtype** identifier **is** subtype_indication ;

subtype_indication ::= type_mark [constraint]

type_mark ::= *type*_name | *subtype*_name

constraint ::= range_constraint
| floating_point_constraint | fixed_point_constraint
| index_constraint | discriminant_constraint

D.2.5 Derived types

derived_type_definition ::= **new** subtype_indication

D.2.6 Scalar types

range_constraint ::= **range** range

range ::= *range*_attribute | simple_expression .. simple_expression

D.2.7 Enumeration types

enumeration_type_definition ::= (enumeration_literal_specification
{, enumeration_literal_specification})

enumeration_literal_specification ::= enumeration_literal

enumeration_literal ::= identifier | character_literal

D.2.8 Integer types

integer_type_definition ::= range_constraint

D.2.9 Real types

real_type_definition ::= floating_point_constraint
  | fixed_point_constraint

floating_point_constraint ::= floating_accuracy_definition
  [range_constraint]

floating_accuracy_definition ::= **digits** *static*_simple_expression

fixed_point_constraint ::= fixed_accuracy_definition
  [range_constraint]

fixed_accuracy_definition ::= **delta** *static*_simpleexpression

D.2.10 Array types

array_type_definition ::= unconstrained_array_definition
  | constrained_array_definition

unconstrained_array_definition ::= **array** (
  index_subtype_definition {, index_subtype_definition})
  of *component*_subtype_indication

constrained_array_definition ::= **array** index_constraint
  of *component*_subtype_indication

index_subtype_definition ::= type_mark **range** <>

index_constraint ::= (discrete_range {, discrete_range})

discrete_range ::= *discrete*_subtype_indication | range

D.2.11 Record types

```
record_type_definition ::=
  record
    component_list
  end record

component_list ::= component_declaration {component_declaration}
  | {component_declaration} variant_part | null ;

component_declaration ::= identifier_list :
  component_subtype_definition [:= expression] ;

component_subtype_definition ::= subtype_indication

discriminant_part ::= ( discriminant_specification {;
  discriminant_specification} )

discriminant_specification ::= identifier_list : type_mark
  [:= expression]

discriminant_constraint ::= ( discriminant_association
  {, discriminant_association} )

discrimination_association ::= [discriminant_simple_name
  { | discriminant_simple_name} =>] expression

variant_part ::=
  case discriminant_simple_name is
      variant
    {variant}
  end case ;

variant ::=
  when choice { | choice} =>
    component_list

choice ::= simple_expression
  | discrete_range | others | component_simple_name
```

D.2.12 Access types

access_type_definition ::= **access** subtype_indication

D.2.13 Incomplete type declarations

incomplete_type_declaration ::=
    type identifier [discriminant_part];

D.2.14 Declarative parts

declarative_part ::= {basic_declarative_item}{later_declarative_item}

basic_declarative_item ::= basic_declaration
    | representation_clause | use_clause

later_declarative_item ::= body
    | subprogram_declaration | package_declaration
    | task_declaration | generic_declaration
    | use_clause | generic_instantiation

body ::= proper_body | body_stub

proper_body ::= subprogram_body | package_body | task_body

D.3 Names and expressions

D.3.1 Names

name ::= simple_name
    | character_literal | operator_symbol
    | indexed_component | slice
    | selected_component | attribute

simple_name ::= identifier

prefix ::= name | function_call

D.3.2 Indexed components

indexed_component ::= prefix (expression {, expression})

D.3.3 Slices

slice ::= prefix (discrete_range)

D.3.4 Selected components

selected_component ::= prefix . selector

selector ::= simple_name
 | character_literal | operator_symbol | **all**

D.3.5 Attributes

attribute ::= prefix ' attribute_designator

attribute_designator ::=
 simple_name [(*universal_static_*expression)]

D.3.6 Aggregates

aggregate ::= (component_association {, component_association})

component_association ::= [choice { | choice} =>] expression

D.3.7 Expressions

expression ::= relation {**and** relation}
 | relation {**and then** relation}
 | relation {**or else** relation}
 | relation {**or** relation}
 | relation {**xor** relation}

relation ::=
 simple_expression [relational_operator simple_expression]
 | simple_expression [**not**] **in** range
 | simple_expression [**not**] **in** type_mark

simple_expression ::=
 [unary_adding_operator] term {binary_adding_operator term}

term ::= factor {multiplying_operator factor}

factor::= primary [** primary] | **abs** primary | **not** primary

primary ::= numeric_literal
| **null** | aggregate | string_literal
| name | allocator | function_call
| type_conversion | qualified_expression | (expression)

D.3.8 Operators

logical_operator ::= **and** | **or** | **xor**

relational_operator ::= = | /= | < | <= | > | >=

binary_adding_operator ::= + | – | &

unary_adding_operator ::= + | –

multiplying_operator ::= * | / | **mod** | **rem**

highest_precedence_operator ::= ** | **abs** | **not**

D.3.9 Type conversions

type_conversion ::= type_mark (expression)

D.3.10 Qualified expressions

qualified_expression ::=
type_mark ' (expression) | type_mark ' aggregate

D.3.11 Allocators

allocator ::= **new** subtype_indication | **new** qualified_expression

D.4 Statements

D.4.1 Simple and compound statements – sequences of statements

sequence_of_statements ::= statement {statement}

statement ::= {label} simple_statement | {label} compound_statement

simple_statement ::= null_statement
| assignment_statement
| exit_statement
| goto_statement
| delay_statement
| raise_statement
| procedure statement
| return_statement
| entry_call_statement
| abort_statement
| code_statement

compound statement ::= if_statement
| case_statement
| block_statement
| select_statement
| loop_statement
| accept_statement

label ::= << *label*_simple_name >>

null_statement ::= **null** ;

D.4.2 Assignment statements

assignment statement ::= *variable*_name := expression ;

D.4.3 If statements

if_statement ::=
if condition **then**
sequence_of_statements
{**elseif** condition **then**
sequence_of_statements}
[**else**
sequence_of_statements]
end if ;

condition ::= *boolean*_expression

D.4.4 Case statements

case_statement ::=
case expression **is**
case_statement_alternative
{case_statement_alternative}
end case ;

```
case_statement_alternative ::=
   when choice { | choice} => sequence_of_statements
```

D.4.5 Loop statements

```
loop_statements ::=
   [loop_simple_name :]
      [iteration_scheme] loop
         sequence_of_statements
      end loop [loop_simple_name] ;

iteration_scheme ::= while condition
   | for loop_parameter_specification

loop_parameter_specification ::=
   identifier in [reverse] discrete_range
```

D.4.6 Block statements

```
block_statement ::=
   [block_simple_name :]
      [declare
          declarative_part]
       begin
          sequence_of_statements
      [exception
          exception_handler
         {exception_handler}]
       end [block_simple_name] ;
```

D.4.7 Exit statements

```
exit_statement ::=
      exit [loop_name] [when condition] ;
```

D.4.8 Return statements

```
return_statement ::= return [expression] ;
```

D.4.9 Goto statements

```
goto_statement ::= goto label_name ;
```

D.5 Subprograms

D.5.1 Subprogram declarations

```
subprogram_declaration ::= subprogram_specification ;

subprogram_specification ::=
    procedure identifier [formal_part]
   | function designator [formal_part] return type_mark

designator ::= identifier | operator_symbol

operator_symbol ::= string_literal

formal_part ::=
    ( parameter_specification {; parameter_specification} )

parameter_specification ::=
   identifier_list : mode type_mark [:= expression]

mode ::= [in] | in out | out
```

D.5.2 Subprogram bodies

```
subprogram_body ::=
   subprogram_specification is
      [declarative_part]
    begin
       sequence_of_statements
   [exception
       exception_handler
      {exception_handler}]
    end [designator] ;
```

D.5.3 Subprogram calls

```
procedure_call_statement ::=
   procedure_name [actual_parameter_part] ;

function_call ::=
   function_name [actual_parameter_part]
```

actual_parameter_part ::=
 (parameter_association {, parameter_association})

parameter_association ::= [formal_parameter =>] actual_parameter

formal_parameter ::= *parameter*_simple_name

actual_parameter ::= expression
 | *variable*_name | type_mark (*variable*_name)

D.6 Packages

D.6.1 Package structure

package_declaration ::= package_specification ;

package_specification ::=
 package identifier **is**
  {basic_declarative_item}
 [**private**
  {basic_declarative_item}]
 end [*package*_simple_name]

package_body ::=
 package body *package*_simple_name **is**
  [declarative_part]
 [**begin**
  sequence_of_statements
 [**exception**
  exception_handler
  {exception_handler}]]
 end [*package*_simple_name] ;

D.6.2 Private types and deferred constant declarations

private_type_declaration ::=
 type identifier [discriminant_part] **is**
  [**limited**] **private** ;

deferred_constant_declaration ::=
 identifier_list : **constant** type_mark ;

D.7 Visibility rules

D.7.1 Use clauses

use_clause ::= **use** *package*_name {, *package*_name} ;

D.7.2 Renaming declarations

```
renaming_declaration ::=
     identifier  :  type_mark  renames  object_name ;
   | identifier  :  exception  renames  exception_name ;
   | package identifier renames  package_name ;
   | subprogram_specification  renames
       subprogram_or_entry_name ;
```

D.8 Tasks

D.8.1 Task specifications and task bodies

task_declaration ::= task_specification ;

```
task_specification ::=
   task [type] identifier [is
      {entry_declaration}
      {representation_clause}
   end [task_simple_name]]
```

```
task_body ::=
   task body  task_simple_name is
      [declarative_part]
   begin
       sequence_of_statements
   [exception
       exception_handler
      {exception_handler}]
   end [task_simple_name] ;
```

D.8.2 Entries, entry calls and accept statements

```
entry_declaration ::=
   entry identifier [(discrete_range)] [formal_part] ;
```

entry_call_statement ::= *entry_*name [actual_parameter_part] ;

accept_statement ::=
  accept *entry_*simple_name [(entry_index)][formal_part][**do**
    sequence_of_statements
  end [*entry_*simple_name]] ;

entry_index ::= expression

D.8.3 Delay statements, duration and time

delay_statement ::= **delay** simple_expression ;

D.8.4 Select statements

select_statement ::= selective_wait
  | conditional_entry_call | times_entry_call

D.8.5 Selective waits

selective_wait ::=
  select
    select_alternative
  {**or**
    select_alternative}
  [**else**
    sequence_of_statements]
  end select ;

select_alternative ::=
  [**when** condition =>]
    selective_wait_alternative

selective_wait_alternative ::= accept_alternative
  | delay_alternative | terminate_alternative

accept_alternative ::= accept_statement [sequence_of_statements]

delay_alternative ::= delay_statement [sequence_of_statements]

terminate_alternative ::= **terminate** ;

D.8.6 Conditional entry calls

```
conditional_entry_call ::=
  select
     entry_call_statement
    [sequence_of_statements]
  else
     sequence_of_statements
  end select ;
```

D.8.7 Timed entry calls

```
timed_entry_call ::=
  select
     entry_call_statement
    [sequence_of_statements]
  or
     delay_alternative
  end select ;
```

D.8.8 Abort statements

abort_statement ::= **abort** *task*_name {, *task*_name} ;

D.9 Program structure and compilation issues

D.9.1 Compilation units – library units

compilation ::= {compilation_unit}

compilation_unit ::= context_clause library_unit
  | context_clause secondary_unit

library_unit ::= subprogram_declaration
  | package_declaration | generic_declaration
  | generic_instantiation | subprogram_body

secondary_unit ::= library_unit_body | subunit

library_unit_body ::= subprogram_body | package_body

D.9.2 Context clauses

context_clause ::= {with_clause {use_clause}}

with_clause ::= **with** *unit*_simple_name {, *unit*_simple_name} ;

D.9.3 Subunits

body_stub ::=
    subprogram_specification **is separate** ;
  | **package body** *package*_simple_name **is separate** ;
  | **task body** *task*_simple_name **is separate** ;

subunit ::= **separate** (*parent_unit*_name) proper_body

D.10 Exceptions

D.10.1 Exception declarations

exception_declaration ::= identifier_list : **exception** ;

D.10.2 Exception handlers

exception_handler ::=
  when exception_choice { | exception_choice} =>
    sequence_of_statements

exception_choice ::= *exception*_name | **others**

D.10.3 Raise statements

raise_statements ::= **raise** [*exception*_name] ;

D.11 Generic units

D.11.1 Generic declarations

generic_declaration ::= generic_specification ;

generic_specification ::=
    generic_formal_ part subprogram_specification
  | generic_formal_part package_specification

generic_formal_part ::= **generic** {generic_parameter_declaration}

generic_parameter_declaration ::=
    identifier_list : [**in** [**out**]] type_mark [:= expression] ;
  | **type** identifier **is** generic_type_definition ;
  | private_type_declaration
  | **with** subprogram_specification [**is** name] ;
  | **with** subprogram_specification [**is** <>] ;

generic_type_definition ::=
  (<>) | **range** <> | **digits** <> | **delta** <>
  | array_type_definition | access_type_definition

D.11.2 Generic Instantiation

generic_instantiation ::=
    package identifier **is**
      new *generic_package_*name
      [generic_actual_part] ;
  | **procedure** identifier **is**
      new *generic_procedure_*name
      [generic_actual_part] ;
  | **function** designator **is**
      new *generic_function_*name
      [generic_actual_part] ;

generic_actual_part ::=
  (generic_association {, generic_association})

generic_association ::=
  [generic_formal_parameter =>] generic_actual_parameter

generic_formal_parameter ::= *parameter_*simple_name
  | operator_symbol

generic_actual_parameter ::= expression
  | *variable_*name |*subprogram_*name | *entry_*name | type_mark

D.12 Representation clauses

D.12.1 Representation clauses

```
representation_clause ::=
    type_representation_clause | address_clause

type_representation_clause ::= length_clause
    | enumeration_representation_clause
    | record_representation_clause
```

D.12.2 Length clauses

```
length_clause ::= for attribute use simple_expression ;
```

D.12.3 Enumeration representation clauses

```
enumeration_representation_clause ::=
    for type_simple_name use aggregate ;
```

D.12.4 Record representation clauses

```
record_representation_clause ::=
    for type_simple_name use
        record [alignment_clause]
            {component_clause}
        end record ;

alignment_clause ::= at mod static_simple_expression ;

component_clause ::=
    component_name at static_simple_expression range
        static_range ;
```

D.12.5 Address clauses

```
address_clause ::= for simple_name use at simple_expression ;
```

D.13 Machine code insertions

```
code_statement ::= type_mark ' record_aggregate ;
```

Index